GW01403001

THE
CLASSICAL POETS

Journal 2016 | Vol. 4 | Edited by Evan Mantyk & Connie Phillips

Classical Poets Publishing

Mount Hope, New York

Coeditors: Evan Mantyk & Connie Phillips
Layout Editor: Diana Benedetti

Inquiries and Membership: submissions@classicalpoets.org

On the Cover Art

"Metamorphosis" by Steven J. Levin

By Neal Dachstadter

A TRAIL that stumbled on a door,
A doubled one, upon a floor,
Some fellow just as you and me,
Approached the portal now we see,

And unobtrusive might have been,
Except he'd shed, down to the skin,
Some aspect of mundanity,
He'd cast away, like vanity.

O was it poor modernity
He'd traded, for eternity?

Table of Contents

How to Turn Around Poetry's Downward Trend

By Evan Mantyk

TODAY, the state of poetry in the general public is such that you might go to a poetry reading at your local library, café, or church and none of the poems read there rhyme. You may also hear no discernable meter. At the same time, the audience of poetry is increasingly dwindling as poetry becomes appealing and understandable only to the poets themselves.

According to the government's *Survey on National Participation in the Arts*, released last year, Americans' reading of literature has stayed static, but reading of poetry has sharply declined. In 1992, 17 percent of Americans said they had read or listened to a poem in the last twelve months, but that figure dropped to a mere 7 percent by 2012, the worst decline of any literary genre. In another decade or two, we are looking at virtual oblivion.

How do we turn around this dismal downward trend? How do we revive poetry—a free or low-cost pastime that stimulates your mind, inspires your soul, satisfies your grandest longings, fortifies the pillars of great civilizations and cultures, and communicates your ideas and feelings more effectively than almost anything else? How do we do it?

The first step, which we have accomplished here, is to return poetry to what people recognize as poetry, in other words, rhyme and meter. Beyond that, I have no definitive answers but only fragments and clues for how we must re-approach poetry and stimulate the regrowth of a non-poet audience for poetry. I will share what I have learned with you. I have a 9-year-old son and a 7-year-old daughter and I've tried numerous poems on them. Funny and humorous poems, and poems marked "children's poetry," sometimes work and sometimes don't. The poems they enjoy most, regardless of poem quality or their particular interest in the subject matter, are riddles. From the Riddler in *Batman* comic books and movies to the riddles of Gollum in *The Hobbit* to the traditional lantern riddles of the Mid-Autumn Festival (the Chinese equivalent of Thanksgiving), riddles are an age-old heritage that is still relevant and engaging today. Riddles make poetry interactive, fun, and relevant to non-poets. If the people want riddles, I say we give them riddles. (I note that in writing riddles too, I have discovered that if you think the riddle is too easy, it is probably just right.)

Recently, I saw Christopher Nolan's movie *Interstellar,* which prominently featured Dylan Thomas's rhyming poem "Do Not Go Gentle Into That Good Night." Here, we have classical poetry being disseminated to and enriching the lives of millions of moviegoers, most of whom are non-poets. At their roots, other artistic fields, such as filmmaking—and perhaps all fields and endeavors in a general sense—could be looked at as extensions of poetry. If you have a solid grasp and understanding of good poetry, the simplest form of artistic communication, then you can utilize that foundational perspective and harness it within whatever field you are in as Nolan has effectively done. In this way too, being a poet is not an end in itself but a bridge to greater achievements in a diverse range of settings.

Lastly, classrooms remain the surest and easiest way to facilitate engagement of non-poets with poetry. To put it more accurately, humanities education itself, including History, Social Studies, and English Language Arts, benefits immensely from the study of poetry. A core skill in these areas is to ascertain meaning and value in a text. Classical poetry provides the perfect grounds for cultivating this skill. It is a forum that balances free-spiritedness, beauty, creativity, and passion with structure, discipline, order, and restraint. Classical poetry offers not only a break from long, dry history texts and uninteresting novels but also a place for honing interpretative, critical reading and intuitive skills. If you are a teacher, consider using more poetry in your classroom. Further, for this reason, we have included a chapter at the end of this year's journal that is essentially a short poetry textbook. It features basic terms for classical poetry; ten great classical poems, including analysis, biographical information, and study questions and activities that go with them; instructions on writing a sonnet that are tiered from beginner level to advanced level; and works that reflect on the state of poetry in today's world, including study questions.

I implore you now, go forth and project the majestic and mysterious forces of classical poetry into the realms that lie before you, with a focus on those multitudes out there who are not poets and who do not usually read poems. They are your future audience.

Godspeed!

Chapter I

Natural Beauty

"Persephone," 2011, oil on linen, by Zarahn Southon.

A Winterberry Sonnet

By John Grey

WINTERBERRY disrupts the frozen curse.
My vision's charmed by tiny blobs of red
Between fine-toothed leaves, above a thick bed
Of snow that baits low branches to immerse
In mounds, but they refute its chill or worse,
Cold's inference that matter should be dead
Or trapped indoors. This brave bush flaunts instead
Its rare December spring, bold universe.

Like holly, I sense bloom in darker thought
That would overwhelm me sure, were there not
Deep in my heart, a priceless maxim taught
By love, to recall what must not be forgot,
That bleakness is mere background, a mind ought
To imitate a winterberry's lot.

The Cherry Blooms in Central Park

By Peter Agnos

IN CENTRAL Park the cherries now
Are hung with blooms along the slough,
And stand around the reservoir,
Pink and white Spring avatars.

Now of my three-score years and ten
I've outlived many better men;
I'm over-the average hill by five....
I wonder why I'm still alive.

To gaze at cherry trees in bloom
One hundred years seems little room—

Maybe one will whisper in my ear
The meaning of the changing year.

Hints from the Moon

By E.P. Fisher

(Monday)

BEGINNING with zero, hints from the moon
Going through phases, ripe in the womb;
Time out of nothing, pared in the night,
Planet of sorrow tilting to light;
Retrograde motion, surf pushed & pulled,
Full moon to crescent, new moon to full…

Lifting & lowering tides in the dark,
Waxing & waning waves in the heart
Breaking & whispering, rhymed in a dream,
Mouth like a river, scenes from the sea;
Emptiness mints its circumference in space,
Coin of the realm, stamped with love's face…

Talisman, amulet, symbol of change,
Harvest of shadows bathing the brain;
Matrix of shape-shifting primitive forms
Curving to crisis—tusk, tooth & horn—
Mimic the rhythm, occult, in eclipse
Image, enigma of time on my lips…

Mirror of madness, omen of blood,
Cycle of heroes, moods of the gods;
Ides interregnum, isle of dead kings,
Midwife to poetry, horses with wings;
Woman of mystery's embryo curled,
Unconscious, cosmic egg of the world.

Touching Bottom

By E.P. Fisher

JUST heard an apple
    In the half dark
Go thump for autumn:
    Plump the sound
Of ground and round fruit
    Touching bottom

The falling planet
    Tumbling down
Eavesdrops on Eden,
    As insect legions
Drum the ear, and deer
    Invade my garden.

The rabbit's bramble
    Underground
Sanctum-sanctorum;
    The raven's mock
Refrain and age-old
    Raucous anthem.

Etched out in shadow
    Phantom limbs
Bruise moons worm-eaten:
    My elbow ghost
Whose taproots plumb
    A lost Elysium.

Just heard the wind blow
    Through the rain
And gain momentum;
    One grief to go,
One leaf remains,
    One frantic pattern.

Spring Tanka

By Brian McCabe

NOW Spring time is here;
Snow drops of white will appear
Behind them will come
Yellow harbingers of sun,
Daffodils of the New Year.

Horses

By Ruth Hill

TELL me what power hits the ground,
heard a mile away, ear to mound?
Earth's tympanic membrane resounds;
like kettle drums, the hoof beat pounds!
Or what, when they run together,
frightens every flight from feather?
Deer run sideways and leave their young;
minnows from shallow creeks are flung.
Wolves cease hunting; lithe lizards hide,
beetles find caves and crawl inside.
Mighty wind dust, kicked up by heels,
mimics thunder and lightning peals.
Muscles ripple, stallions cripple;
whinnies, neighing, snorting, triple.
Tell me how, when they're wild and free,
they turn and run and come to me?
Then tame and lame and docile bow,
to man's child. Can you tell me how?

Godsong

By Ruth Hill

NO MUSIC made by human hand
can match an orchestra this grand,
as I recline in forest glade
to hear the songs that God has made.

Brooks' sweet babble alone can soothe;
background breezes so subtly smooth.
Species of songbirds on parade;
rattles of aspen leaves are made.

While silent clouds are tumbling by:
the piercing shriek of Flickers' cry.
Woodpecker drums while Rufus hums,
and bees make love to chrysanthemums.

Squirrels titter, clunk nut litter.
Brown beaver chews to spread the news:
soon trout will rise to buzzing flies,
and frogs will croak on air they choke.

Rushes rub like scouring brushes;
the crickets sing to evening bring.
The sky gets dark; a hush below…
satisfied, I must sadly go.

Storyteller

By Michael Harmon

We sit around the fire.
The storyteller drones,
until his words expire
in silence like the stones.
Primeval darkness frames
the flower-yellow flames

enlightening our faces.
Like breeze-blown blossoms, we
shift mutely in our places
within the ring while he,
as yellow flowers fail,
resumes again his tale,

which seems to have no end.
Or we may wish it so.
His words bloom and transcend
the darkness that we know
and, through descending night,
bring on another light

to follow, leading to
a place we can survive,
and our own dark subdue.
His words keep us alive,
and, like the dawn, display
the flowers of our day.

To a Beech

By Hugh Rose

SPREAD twig fingers.
 Shed your leaves.
Those that linger:
 They may grieve
When comes the winter
 But, come spring
New buds splinter,
 New blooms bring
That grow and swell
 Concentric bands
That breathe and dwell
 Upon this land.

Plumb the darkness.
 Glory light.
Show us far less
 Than you might.
Keep us guessing
 Of your roots.
Don't confess in
 Subtle shoots.
Paint the sky
 With each green brush.
When the sun dies
 Sweep on dusk.

Still and still,
 And still more still.
Silent, grand,
 And so tranquil.
Show me I
 Have stillness too,

Buried by my
   Need to do.
To do, to speak,
   To color in,
To fill the bleak
   Wide space within
With sound and noise
   And thought and speech;
With any toys
   Within my reach.

Teach me instead
   To stand and be;
To leave my head
   And sit in me.
Teach me to make
   A home for those
Who fear and quake
   From unseen foes.
Teach me to celebrate
   The earth,
And not debate
   Its cost or worth.
Teach me to love
   All those below,
All those above,
   All that I know.

Sonnet on a Supermodel

By Maya Sokolovski

THOU airbrushed beauty of saintly deeds
    Winking glibly from the page
Desire, ardor, envy feeds
    The mag a stand-in for a stage.

Your face adorns walls, billboards, ads
    Dear features always saying "YES"
The whole world loves you, as it stands
    Yet what you know we only guess.

The girl—you—walking down the road
    Hair mussed, no makeup, a plain white tee
You step out the store with a heavy load
    Then stop, and look; then you see me.

I see the warmth within your soul
It is the mark of someone whole.

Desert Storm, Prairie Lines

By Neal Dachstadter

STREAM and river, reservoir
Gleaming color, desert floor,
Sky of rain and buxom cloud,
Fiery vein and thunder proud,
Storm benign of lake rebirth,
Farm and wine and break of mirth,
Alarm of kine and slake of Earth,
Form divine mid aching dearth.

Poplars

By Neal Dachstadter

TONES of the wind, and words of the tree,
Stirring and blending, applauding in key,
New-finished leaves, descending in green:
Unblemished sheaves, extended in Spring.

Sedona

By Elizabeth Spencer Spragins

(A Welsh Rhupunt)

DEEP shadows fade
Red rock cascade
To purpled jade—
Sun sparks ignite.

Stone sentries stare
Sightless through air
At treadless stair
Spanning the height.

No mortals dare
Enter the lair
Or linger where
Spirit meets sprite.

This shrine of stone
And bleached white bone
Hides secrets shown
In the moonlight.

Meditating

By Colin Fredericson

THROUGH sandy, muddy, rocky creek,
Silted, crudded, hard to speak,
My heart was heavy, worn, and cramped,
I needed someplace I could camp.

Nature spoke, I took the chance
To venture out with shield and lance
A trek that took me into night
Parched and filthy, sworn to fight

Until I thought I found a clue,
A mountain peak I thought I knew,
A place of peace to meditate,
With quiet winds and tranquil lakes.

Was this the place I sought to reach?
The one where Wukong* bit the peach?
Still, relaxed, no words to say
Pesky thoughts were miles away.

Wukong: The Monkey King, a famous hero and spiritual cultivator in classical Chinese literature.

One Summer Day

By Martin Elster

An allusion to Beethoven

WHILE walking through the woods one summer day,
    he glanced along a river, clear and bright,
saw bubbling notes like dappled fish at play,
    and dashed them off that night by candlelight.
Meandering down coniferous-scented trails
    where chickadees and tree frogs made such noise,
he didn't hear a thing except the scales
    and chords and cadences that were his toys.
He couldn't hear the leaves in the aspen thickets,
    the deer flies buzzing round his graying hair,
the sound of countless madly rasping crickets,
    nor the peals of far-off thunder in the air.

Yet who can miss those leaves, that summer breeze,
that river rushing through his symphonies?

The Inward Light

By Ann Keith

BE PROOF against the eye and ear
And every sense that stultifies
The inward light, supreme, austere,
The keenly sharp, the keenly clear,
That by the lucent beam it darts
Illuminates the deepest hearts.

Sonnet on Discernment

By Ann Keith

ALL varied lengths and waves are there: The ear
Receives their tones; the soul perceives and weighs
Each separate shade of light and sound that plays
Upon it subtly in the atmosphere.

Become discerning slowly by severe
Self-discipline, it isolates the rays
Of beneficial influence and obeys
Their summons and endeavors to draw near.

Desiring always purity, release
From bonds and false misshapings that decrease
The vigor of its vision, as a flower
Turns to the sun, the soul must never cease
To move towards that source of radiant peace
That draws it steadily at every hour.

Dawn on the Shore

By Ann Keith

AN HOUR before the dawn of day,
I walked beside the tranquil bay,
   Along the sandy shore.

The air was still. The wind had ceased.
The planet Venus hung in the east,
   In the west the moon sank lower.

The tide was down, the sands outspread;
I walked with Orion above my head;
   Pale crabs flashed up before

My feet, like flitting ghosts, and fled,
Flickered and darted and skimmed and sped
   Back to the shadows once more.

I walked beside the still sea, thinking
Of all the things I loved, and linking
   My future and my past,

Walked and watched my shadow glide
Along the wet sands at my side.
   The water became one vast

And gently heaving opaline mass,
Perfectly calm and smooth as glass.
   The sun, still hidden, cast

Its light before it. The ocean wore
A luminous luster long before
   It rose from the sea at last.

Then, layer by layer, the veils were withdrawn.
Sea and hills took shape in the dawn
   And the sails of the small boats, white

Specks on the clear expanse of blue.
Fresh blossoms globed with morning dew
   Are not more fresh and bright

Than the trees and rocks and hills of that bay,
Emerging into the dawning day,
   Out of the chaos of night.

Entranced and rapt, I lingered there,
Breathing in the crystal air,
   Lapped in calm delight.

So deep was the spell that I felt my own
Bodily substance of blood and bone,
   Muscle and nerve and vein,

Transformed in their nature and drifted away
Over the sea to the rim of the day.
    No limits could now retain

My spirit. I felt it lift and rise
Like vaporous mist that mounts up through the skies
    After a passing rain.

In that hour of peace beside the sea,
The gods made recompense to me
    For many hours of pain.

Rare Dreams

By Dean Robbins

I'M LOOKING through the window of a plane
in which I've never been, nor ever will;
staring beyond a wing that is not there
into a sky I've never seen nor care
to see again; above clouds strangely still,

dropping a soft and steady soothing rain
upon the midnight silent house below,
in which I lie still as those clouds—rare dreams
in which I know nothing is as it seems,
hearing the drizzle outside my window.

Annual

By Dean Robbins

I'VE tied the rose bush to a fanned arbor
  and bled my hands for the trouble
of reaching where thorns offer no harbor,
  and all knots tied must be double.

Ever the price for hands aching to hold
  beauty necessary as breath;
fleeting, fragile, far too willing to fold
  in acceptance of yearly death.

Meditating in the Night

By Daniel Magdalen

THE moon, surrounded by gray lands
    with floating hills and cliffs of clouds,
Spreads fields of light that fade away
    upon the drifting misty shrouds.
The lonely park in stillness waits,
    its blooming trees in dreams all rest,
But now, a gentle breeze comes by
    to whisperingly greet a guest...

Amid the mild silver glow upon her
    cast by night's pale sun,
With velvet steps, a girl arrives;
    The full moon shines as rain clouds run.
Like flowers blossoming, her moves
    make gloom and solitude disperse,
Her legs in lotus folded tight,
    in meditation to immerse.

The graceful figure of the girl
    is wreathed in the translucent tide,
While on the waters of the pond,
    her mirrored solemn postures glide.
A timeless presence of high realms,
    whose statues sit in ancient shrines,
The Buddha's image, through her face,
    in pure ethereal light shines…

The Stairway

By Daniel Magdalen

YOUR spirit's eyes, now opened, see
    The timeless steps of stone ahead…
Old debts weigh down your weakened knee,
    Each step, a human burden's shed.

While slogging up the sacred blocks,
    This trying but fulfilling climb
Casts off the sinfully wrought locks
    To your soul's roots sealed off in time.

The closer to the top you get,
    The narrower this stairway feels.
No more, though, is your mind beset
    By gusts of grief, from which man reels.

Keep high your gaze, for down below
    Death's gaping precipice awaits…
In emptiness… atop… you flow
    Toward bright worlds blooming, past sky's gates.

The Seasons

By Janice Canerdy

EACH season comes with unique threats and majesty;
each plays its role in Nature's year-long pageantry.

As Nature sends spring flowers, autumn leaves,
soft breezes, sunshine, and refreshing rain,
she also rages through with floods and grieves
with droughts and winter storms. She will retain
her power to engender joy and pain.

Seasons

By Ben Zwycky

FORESTED deep purity
   Dusted with a winter's glow;
Crystalline perpetuity
   Takes its place in nature's show.

Fresh sunlight plays with diamonds soft
   That glisten as they sing
In silent awe that drifts aloft
   A peaceful offering.

Great ice sheets yield to spring's sweet kiss
   And snow gives way to rain;
Arboreal chants blend fragrant mists
   That flood the fertile plain.

New fauna dance with life unbound
   And quiver as they sleep,
Loathe to miss one sight or sound,
   Or lose one joy so deep.

Streams trickle, tumbling, giggling down
    And nourish all they meet;
Young bucks do battle with their crowns,
    Their heroes to unseat.

Fierce summer heat strips arid earth
    Of all that's failed to thrive;
Refreshing flows gain countless worth
    For all to stay alive.

Massed Shady greens turn mighty light
    Into life's currency;
Frantic deals done day and night
    In this dependency.

Old summer takes his bow in style
    With whirls of amber shades.
Harvests picked and safely piled
    As daily brightness fades.

Most heed the warnings in the sky
    Of winter's coming wrath:
In insulated sanctuary lie
    Or take a southward path.

And so the cycle runs again
    It's glorious phases through;
Enjoy their transient beauty, then,
    And savor them anew.

The First Day of Spring

By Lorna Davis

THE first day of spring started rainy and cold,
But new greens were sprouting, defiant and bold,
And daffodils nodded their bright heads of gold,
    To make the day not quite as dreary.

As I, winter-weary, looked out through the glass
And wondered if ever this winter would pass,
A rainbow of songbirds alit on the grass
    And watching them, soon I grew cheery.

On closer inspection, I noticed the gray
Was lighter, and brighter indeed was the day,
As the storm clouds were parting and drifting away,
    And sunlight began to break through.

And then, as I watched, winter's grip on the world
Was loosened, as though its cold fingers uncurled,
And outside my window the spring was unfurled
    In a glittering light on the dew.

Taking leave of my window, I stepped to the door,
And into the garden I went, seeking more
Of the warmth that all winter I'd been longing for,
    And out in the sunlight I stood.

The air was still cool, but it smelled fresh and clean,
And the tips of the branches were all dipped in green.
Wherever I looked, signs of spring could be seen,
    And on such days—oh yes—life is good!

The Magic Hour

By Kathy Figueroa

IT'S called "the magic hour"
    Before the sun sinks low
When everything is bathed
    In a warm, golden glow

Colors look much richer
    Flowers, more velveteen
And a country garden
    Is a haven of green

The dragonflies hover
    As light glints on their wings
Tree frogs start their chorus
    And sing of peaceful things

Freedom of Winter Hills

By Matthew Walton / High School Poet

YOU start before the world,
    Beating the sun to the skyline,
Something is waiting for you,
    Just ahead of this incline.
Nothing else is moving,
    Birds silenced by the snow,
The way life should be,
    The best nature can bestow.
Like swimming, like flying,
    The rushing through your hair,
That sweet sense of movement,
    Without going anywhere.

With your own path to follow,
    And your own fate to choose,
Just point your skis downhill,
    And you have nothing to lose.

Riverside

By Jarrett Mohn / High School Poet

SUN rays glisten
    Reflect the river;
I stand and listen,
    Can't help but shiver.

Restless fish swim,
    Graceful, majestic,
Watching sunlight dim,
    Thoughts are monolithic.

Nature's beauty endless
    Never ceases to amaze;
I stand still, breathless
    Caught up in a daze.

When Fairies Stop Hiding

By Pamela Corbett

IT'S at the end of the day,
    but it's not over just yet—
It's time for young fairies,
    to grow wings and get wet.
Sneaking out to the sky,
    while the sun descends down—
Creating color for rainbows—
    before the rains hit ground.
Dusk is their favorite time,
    when the day turns dark—
Time to fly to the stars,
    and ignite their blue spark.
In between day and night,
    both a beginning and end—
For they love granting wishes,
    hiding in gardens they tend.

On Rossetti's "Sea Spell"

By Ella Nowicki

HER paper-pliant wrists sink, weighed in air,
as her thumb ends its sojourn on augmented strings
and a sea bleached nail strikes the strands of kings
with the claret tartness of her shaded hair.

Darkest Before Dawn

By Jason W. Larsen

THE sorrows of many pulls upon heart strings
To accomp'ny angelic voices that sing;
Voices so sweet but pain too intense to soothe;
Roads traveled so rough only time's sands can smooth;
No chariot to ride, worn feet wear no shoes;
Seems no choice left to make but still we must choose;
Don't succumb to pain always refuse to lose.

Just as before we walk we learned how to fall;
Can't stand any more? Then remember to crawl;
Listen to the angels they're singing your song,
"Pain is only temporal it won't last long;
You can pass the test it shall help make you strong;
Don't feel so alone we are here all along;
Do the best that you can and nothing is wrong."

Let harmonious voices return your feet;
Hit the ground running from the jaws of defeat;
Survive the night and a new dawn will arrive,
In a flash of brilliance you finely realize,
It always seems darkest before the sunrise;
Feel the sunshine and wipe the tears from your eyes;
Watch as dawn's grandeur reveals a blessed surprise.

Lives I Have Survived

By Damian Robin

AS I was flying high and looking down,
   the lonely regent of my tiny crown
in one-dimension's cold and breath-thin air,
   anxiously intent on prey down there,
I'd had enough of limit's lonely plains,
   the flat dimensions where my kingdom reigns,
the mumbled tastes and smells I'd feel and "see"
   within the fat of corporeality,
and fed up with an empty stomach's need
   of staying calm and poised in hunger-greed
of scouring earth and heaven for a feed
   and of the pumping species' lust to breed
and being just the slight of something more,
   the flight of fancy or the metaphor
of some small god or spirit I might be
   enbarbed into this bird-brained vanity,
I craved a warmth and blood but not to eat;
   I longed for solid earth and solid feet
the camaraderie of group and herd,
   not the cramps of solitary bird;
for squeezed within this single animal,
   I felt my spirit growth was minimal,
two forward eyes formed cross wires for one shot
   with single-minded thoughts towards that shot
no sense of "love" towards my hunter kind,
   just single thoughts within a single mind,
no sense of multiple or larger heart,
   just the calculating killer's art
I held vestigial memories of "loves,"
   but felt harsh hawk affinities to doves
I had ideas and knew compassion's frame
   like empty victim bones without a name;

my fuller heart's desire for kindred flesh,
   where individuality can mesh
with individuality and more
   was not a place I sensed my wings could soar;
the levels I could climb felt limited
   and many planes are only passed when dead
and dead again one finds another plane
   and cleans the mind but still there's matter's stain.
In ways predestined helpers have contrived
   I'm made aware of lives I have survived;
I know there's more to me than just one time
   that even birds can conscience the sublime
and while the air around me frictions heat,
   my wings get heavier and cease to beat;
I feel a future where my wings are feet
   and I jostle with thick-bodied meat;
I feel the whole of me come down to earth
   a loss, a fall—I wouldn't call it birth—
a drop through branches that I cannot stop;
   the holding sense of present does not stop;
my feathers shrink to single spines of hair
   now clumps of ear start sprouting where none were;
what remains of talons grab on grass
   and swelling sinew atoms start to pass
through moon-spaced eyes to seeing skins of deer,
   four-hoofed and heavy weighted hard to steer;
a double helix seed in me unchains;
   I'm galloping while tissue type constrains,
fixed in muscle-stretching entropy,
   pumping veins so big so odd so free,
bumping into others without slipping.
   We flood the plain our hooves are hardly gripping,
ignoring fear retreating is no use,
   wild and deer with freedom rushing loose;
I stumble, huddle, gushing, flushing, flinging,
   a streaming herd of steaming heart-beats winging.

Choice

By Damian Robin

NOW to change;
rise to rearrange;
fix buckled tracks; iron out the cracked strange.

Time to take
off the human make-
up, look within and see beyond the fake:

catch and count
seeds in the air; mount
heaven's stairs; stay aware; stay calm; pipe

fountains from seas;
drop tears under trees;
don't be diverted by balmy follies;

and make sure
your next best thing—boring,
challenging, bland, hit, miss, grand—is pure.

Chapter II

Humor & Riddles

"A Teasing Riddle," by August Leopold Egg (1816–1863)

Ideology

By Robert King

IDEOLOGY is a disease,
 Impervious to reason,
An infection known to seize
 One in the election season.

It has alas no known cure,
 This paralysis of the brain,
No thought is allowed to stir
 If it runs against the grain.

Left untreated it will spread
 Far and wide o'er the land,
Undefeated until at last instead
 Another ideology raises its hand.

For treatment, what can one do?
 Prescribe an enema every day
So that when their crap they spew,
 The toilet sweeps it all away.

Igor at the Kitchen Sink

By Alecsei Durbew

I SAW him washing dishes at the sink.
 He stood against the smooth, white countertop,
and tan, wood cabinet below his pink
 thick, stalwart legs—bull in a china shop.
O, he was not Prince Hamlet at the court,
 but rather more Prince Omelette or Prince Ham,
more like a chef than chief at Agincourt,

more like a servant, serf, or serving man.
But he worked hard, clench, scrub, rinse and release,
    clench, scrub, rinse and release, again, again,
as if in some grand, mesmerizing piece
    some mad, Romantic pianist had penned.

I wondered what would happen to that stack—
o, as he washed—would all the dishes crack?

A South African Riddle

By Basil Fillis

THE tabular splendor stands with pride
    between the lion's head and Devil's peak,
where you can fly on the Northern side;
    when a Southern pleasure you may seek.

*Answer on page 180

On Volkswagen's Emission Scandal

By Tony Henderson

LIES and half-truths? Daily fayre
But for pious folk it's only fair
If you peddle wares upon our trust,
When you're caught you should be bust.

Someone must have made the call
To tweak the needle just to fall
Below the threshold, no alarm,
Thus put our lives in deadly harm.

Was it like King Henry's piece?
Rid me of this turbulent priest?
Or was it devious local crew?
Who'll take the rap from cold HQ?

"The Boss has gone, if he's not wise
A fool be he, but no surprise!"
Those that are left face their doom:
A perfect fart; a crowded room.

A Fifteen-Year-Old's Response to Frost

By Janice Canerdy

"This 'pome' don't make NO sense! What junk!"
    the scowling students muttered.
"Two roads in the woods!" one hissed. "Such bunk"
    opinions rudely uttered.

I quelled the urge to hurl my book.
    I said, "Can't you surmise
what they might mean? Let's take a look.
    What might they symbolize?"

One hand shot up—then two—then three!
    My probing did the trick.
Alas! Two kids just had to pee.
    The other whined, "I'm sick."

The bell rang. As my prisoners fled,
    "Essays next week," I screamed.
"I ain't no good at them," some said.
    My mind was gone, it seemed.

To Hell with the Hoi Polloi

By Craig Kurtz

TO HELL with the hoi polloi, I say,
democracy is démodé;
aristocrats, by troth, know best,
who needs a scurvy IQ test?
A pox upon the under-class,
salute the King and raise a glass;
the Devil take the working poor;
equality's a royal bore.
What good are beggars who can't laugh,
let's legislate against riff-raff;
the law should puff up the beau monde
and drag the rest through the horse pond.
Good breeding is the source of wit
and should be governed by permit;
the commoners have no éclat
and ought to be against the law.
We'll warrant silks, perruques and dice
'cause being rich is the best vice;
the masses want life more humane,
but why waste all that good champagne?
Let's sign a formal declaration
that makes laboring high treason;
at the risk of being rigid,
wages are prohibited.
Utopia's a bellyache,
let 'em eat cake, for Heaven's sake;
noblesse oblige takes us so far
and then it's time for caviar.

We'll have no revolution, thanks,
'cause freedom's just for Mountebanks;
the House of Bourbon had it right,

the rabble should be more polite.
To hell with the hoi polloi, I say,
gentility has more cachet;
all power to the monarchy,
long live entitled foppery!

Ten Riddles

By Mike Munsell

1.

THE prankster's favorite home decor,
Clockwise or counter, the choice is yours.
Never eaten, found in bowls.
Around I go, I'm on a roll.
What am I?

2.

A FLIGHTLESS bird, born in the east.
I do not chirp, molt or feast.
Stationery, at peace, unmoving if released.
What am I?

3.

AN OVERWHELMING feeling of glum,
A group of men that likes to drum,
Above you many days a year,
Plural, it's music to your ears.
What is it?

4.

MY FAMILY is a handful, and I'm known as the brawler.
I'm the first in order, though my siblings stand taller.
When I'm on my own it can mean one of two things:
Catch me when I'm down and you may frown.
When I'm up, it's a definite yup.

5.

I CAN be hard to find, even when close by.
If you need a fix, I'm your guy.
You'll see right through me,
When you look into my eye.
Who or What am I?

6.

I'M OLD school.
I spent decades in black and white.
Use me gently or you'll get nipped by my sound-bite.
Use me up, and you'll end up with dust.
What am I?

7.

ITCHING to escape
From a dark and drafty place,
Gone in the blink of an eye
Feeling blessed as I float by
What am I?

8.

I DON'T curse, but I swear.
Take a sip, I'm in the air.
What am I?

9.

HIDDEN in your closet
Sits a calcium deposit,
Gutless but not spineless,
Supportive, and yet mindless.
What is it?

10.

TWO characters in a childhood song.
Side by side, we play along.
Spinning, skipping, jumping tracks.
Handled gently, burned in stacks.

*Answers on page 180

Three Riddles

By Damian Robin

1.

IT SHOWS many sides
but usually 2—
can boil & bluster
& end in a stew—
can be clear as crystal
& cut a sharp view—
or narrow to nothing
but be taken as true

2.

I CAN fly
I can make crowds roar
I can pass by
beside, behind, before

I get caught in nets
but seldom in the sea
I cause regrets
and ecstasy

3.

A HOLE in the ground
(usually round)
not
straight
down
like
a well—
straight ahead, on the level, to help people
travel.

*Answers on page 180

Political Banter

By Alan W. Jankowski

ONCE again it's that time of year,
    When political banter seems the rage.
When otherwise normal people,
    Try to come off as some worldly sage.

I have friends who are really nice folks,
    Any other time of the year.
But, once they start with the political rants,
    I really don't want them near.

Of course, their views are always right,
    How could it be any other way?
And you too could be right like them,
    If you just listen to what they say.

Some people take it all quite seriously,
    And engage in rather spirited exchange.
As if convincing all their Facebook friends,
    Will bring about a world of change.

But the more I hear all this political banter,
    The more it makes me think.
That the only party I want to join,
    Is one where I can get a drink.

Arrested by the Grammar Police

By Alan W. Jankowski

IT SEEMS that lately I can't get no peace,
From all those so-called Grammar Police,
Who for some reason think that I should care,
The difference between there, they're and their.

They want to analyze everything I say,
Just waiting for me to lie when I want to lay,
And I really think they just do it because,
They want to further some petty cause.

So, what I do is I mess with there head,
I write the word red when I really mean read,
And I couldn't care less if they throe a fit,
Should I confuse the words elicit with illicit.

And it really don't phase me if I'm derelict,
By writing something like "cause and affect,"
I'll just stare and say "Whatcha gonna do?"
If I want to write that the sky is blew.

Though I really shutter at the very thought,
I'll try to be discrete and not get caught,
But if they should arrest me and throe me in jail,
Just bee sure and come and post my bale.

Beneath the Mask

By Rick Blum

A MASK is worn to hide one's face
from the surly light of day,
but if you open up your mind,
you'll see masks another way.

Zorro donned black mask and cape,
    disguised in cowboy chicness.
Superman, with chiseled jaw,
    hid behind his meekness.

Mascara is a kind of mask,
    designed to cloak eyelashes.
It's often laded-on to lure
    a hunky guy who mashes.

Macho men feel masculine,
    pecs oiled to a gleam,
though mostly it describes a ruse
    to veil low self-esteem.

Masking tape is man's best friend,
    protecting precious borders;
it's not too sticky, tears with ease,
    just what the paint doc orders.

When a clerk hears *Where's damask?*
    from a lady prone to preen,
he knows she seeks the fabric aisle,
    not stuff for Halloween.

A masquerade's a fancy dance
    of character inventions
and a foul façade to hide a soul
    of sinister intentions.

Chief Masconomet never wore
    a mask as far as we can tell,
unlike the Iroquois who thought
    wood ones would make them well.

A mascot is a sprite team pet,
    contrived to bring good luck;
too often played by carefree coeds,
    prone to run amuck.

So now, you see, to find a mask
　　you needn't be a sleuth;
they're everywhere you dare to look,
　　and that's the unmasked truth

Twenty Riddles

By Evan Mantyk

I.

I MAY not have a large population
Compared to China or the United States,
But more than those two or any nation
I've more coastline and freshwater supplies.
What country am I?

II.

THE Earth's final battle ground here unfurled,
According to one ancient prophecy,
It now refers to the end of the world,
It starts with "arm" but ends with no mercy.
What word am I?

III.

THIS one day is as dark as it is bright;
If you are in the southern hemisphere
And it is getting colder now each night,
Then it must be it's this day of the year
What day and month of the year am I?

IV.

WITH the Pharaoh hot on his Hebrew tail,
Moses saw no other option ahead,

The waters raged but the Jews had no sail,
So he parted what sea and onward led?

V.

IF A man named Saturday, on Sunday
Meets a man named Tuesday for a Brunch
But it gets postponed till they meet Thursday,
Who gets them to agree instead to lunch.
On what day do they eat?

VI.

HE DEFEATED the giant named Goliath
And in that battle's triumphant aftermath,
He composed many famous songs or psalms
And by his star still Hebrew hearts enthralls.
Who is he?

VII.

MISS Yellow and Miss White were feeling blue
When they met Miss Orange and Miss Black,
Orange green with envy, White red with shame;
Which secondary color didn't I name?

VIII.

RED was having a good time with Yellow
Until Orange showed up and Red turned pale;
Yellow left, Blue came to say hello.
After Blue left, Green shows up without fail.
What colors are left?

IX.

THE crust of the earth may be cool and tough
And its inside may be warm red liquid,

And above it a layer of white, but not fluff,
For it's not earth that I've got in my head.
What is it?

X.

I AM long, sometimes fat and sometimes thin,
Sometimes bumpy and sometimes very smooth,
And I have many living creatures within,
Float on me and your troubles I will soothe.
What am I?

XI.

SO THIN a slice of salty sustenance,
One bite leaves the taste buds in rapt suspense
Oh Earthen fruit, when'll the next crunch commence?
What am I?

XII.

A PART of a book, a hair off a tree,
Come to my hot tub, I'll make you some tea!
What am I?

XIII.

ONE angry morning after Seven ate Nine,
Mad Three said, "I don't know what Five is for,"
And One said, "Zero is getting too out of line,"
When bad feelings multiply, who can keep score?
What is the sum total of the number sounds in this riddle?

XIV.

THE two of us ate meals totaling three;
The four of them ate one meal for free;

If all six together each ate one meal more,
Minus one who said his belly was sore,
What then is the total meal eaten score?

XV.

I'M A foul creature and I'm feeling down,
And yet my hard mouth never shows a frown;
Maybe I just don't like the cold weather,
I have heard that down south it is better.
What am I?

XVI.

FILL me up, and I'll never leak,
Write me your secrets, I'll never speak;
I don't claim to have a poet's mind,
But I always have an extra line.
What am I?

XVII.

I AM like a really small city;
I often even have my own Subway;
Although I don't have a street, grass or tree,
I have plenty of walkways,
I don't have many shops like a mall
Yet my selection is biggest of all.
What am I?

XVIII.

I HAVE a bottom but no top;
Near the sea is my great castle
I helped build, now it's a hassle:
Threats to destroy it never stop.
What am I?

XIX.

THE first to make it by sea to Asia,
I sailed right around the Cape of Good Hope
Columbus thought that he had found India,
But it was my Portuguese sail and rope.
Who am I?

XX.

I'M THE God of War, I fly through the night,
I'm your neighbor but I'm far away,
I'm a tinge of orange, but mostly white,
You cannot see me during the day,
What am I?

*Answers on page 180

Behind Times

By Karlee Renkoski

THEY tweet like a bird, have books of your face, and Kindle
who?
I can hardly remember which TV button to touch.
I simply don't understand how to google or text you,
or send instant telegrams in seconds; it's just too much!
So, it's better if I keep to my newspapers and such.

Billy Cat and Max Dog

By Don Shook

BURROWED down in leaves of brown
   piled by the garden wall,
our Billy cat dreamed of a rat
   he'd chased down through the hall.
Up from the creek came Max the dog,
   exhausted from his run,
but hearing purring at the wall
   resolved to have some fun.
So with a most ferocious growl
   he charged in fierce delight,
awakening the lazy thing
   who hastily took flight.
With dry leaves rising in his wake,
   Bill scaled that garden wall,
in such a way that others say
   seemed little feat at all.
But Max, unable to slow down
   and thus abort attack,
slid through the leaves like rows of sheaves
   and hit the wall *kerwhack*!
Now Billy from his perch on high
   seemed vaguely unconcerned,
the staggering pooch providing proof,
   a lesson had been learned.
So Billy licked a paw or two
   and curled up quite content;
the purring cat concluding that
   the day had been well spent.

The Brown Dog Tried
to Cross Sixth Street

By Peter Agnos

THE brown dog tried to cross Sixth Street
on his little padded feet;
A Ford hit him! Squashed him flat_____.
So for that dog: that was that.

He'll never cross Sixth Street again.
He'll cross no streets at all.
He'll gnaw no more on chicken bones
nor pee against the wall.

BOW-WOW, BOW-WOW, BOW-WOW, WOW,
    WOW(2x)

He'll no more on a lamb-chop chew,
Nor trip the mailman's feet.
Nor drool on the New York Review,
Nor squat on Seventh Street.

He'll swim no more off Coney Isle,
Nor jog in Central Park,
Nor scan the crowd for a wayward smile
Nor at policemen bark.

BOW-WOW, BOW-WOW, BOW-WOW, WOW,
    WOW(2x)

He'll never wag his tail again;
He's finished with life's farce.
He'll no more shake his grungy mane,
Nor lick a puppy's arse.

The brown dog tried to cross Sixth Street
on his little padded feet;
A Ford hit him! Squashed him flat_____.
So for that dog: that was that.

BOW-WOW, BOW-WOW, BOW-WOW, WOW,
    WOW(4x)

Atlasusa

By Skip Hughes

THE postal gurus are creative and clever.
Our Massachusetts-Pennsylvania family
Brought forth a Maine addition—MA & PA, and ME.
Per partly pluperfect plus purely preposterous purpose,
State names will be spelled with two letters forever.
Of course Hawaiians say "Aloha," meaning HI!
Ohio—OH, and here's a great idea—why
Not unify city and state names? That shouldn't perturb us.

A modest proposal? Think swiftly. For instance,
Try Providenceri, and Walla Wallawa;
Consider Bogalusala, la-la, la, la.
An Idaho robot could be Pocotelloid-created.
Those dogs in New Jersey are sick with Cape Maynj, gents.
Fargond is way out there in North Dakota found.
Kentucky jazzy tunes are Lexingtonky sound.
All hail Oklahoma composer, Hobartok restated.

Mom's line-dancing Georgians Maconga, by jingo.
Talkeetnaak—an Alaskan skill; a paradigm,
Accomplishing both oral functions at one time.
White bears air-defensive at Kodiakak in Alaska?
A Chicagoil—Illinois moll, in the lingo.
Same state—the city finger fashion—Urbanail.

Same state again—my sibling princess—Ciceroil?
Stack toys on display shelves in mid-California—Stocktonca.

Oh fly me to Michigan—Kalamazoomi.
"Let's buy an easy-riding Iowa sports car, Dad."
"I hear that those are made in Davenportia, lad."
Salemma defines Massachusetts, not so as to please ya.
"Go hunting in Maine? Don't you dare Cariboume,
'Cause we New Yorkers have this Lackawannany."
That college town in Iowa? The folks, you see,
Forever forgetting the "n" in it, call it Amesia.

Missouri, let's Rollamo. Just a suggestion.
Hawaii's altitude dilemma—Hilohi?
Wyoming's curiosity—Chugwaterwy?
It sounds like, in Maine, they don't like a big eater—Bangorme.
Some Utahns are crazy. They're nuts, beyond question,
Especially in Loganut and Ogdenut.
You may have heard of New York bison sausage, but—
No matter how thin you might slice it, it's pure Buffalony.

Chapter III
The Cancer
of Terrorism

"St. Michael the Archangel," by Guido Reni (1575–1642)

The Last Column

By Ron L. Hodges

Lines inspired by the 9/11 Memorial

A SHAFT of steel rises erect
its dappled surface all bedecked
small reminders for all who come
this was and is the last column.

After the soaring spires were wrecked,
into madness the heroes trekked.
Their sacrifice, a gruesome sum,
is blazoned on the last column,

a sight that sears us with respect,
a sight that prods us to reflect:
when terror dropped its wicked plumb,
most nobly stood the last column.

But chaos had an architect,
a hate that grows if left unchecked.
Still pounding on a martial drum
they vilify the last column.

These tyrants of a hateful sect
both liberty and life reject,
and lest to them our world succumb
we must arise, the last column.

Is It ISIS or ISIL?

By Robert King

Is it ISIS or ISIL?
I think it is the latter
It really doesn't matter
True, ISIS rhymes with crisis
Let's not lose our heads about this
But ISIL rhymes with evil
And also with the devil

So if reason still prevails
The devil's in the details.

Counterfeit Martyrdom

By Basil Fillis

EVIL terrorists 'round the world
    Reject God's law, "Thou shalt not kill."
Minds indoctrinated, furled
    up in a cold and savage will!

Real martyrs are the brave who die
    adhering to their faith and creed.
Suicide is murder high
    in cowardice, which marks this breed.

Vile murders indiscriminate
    —the innocent among their own—
prove their deeds deliberate;
    an evil doctrine cast in stone!

True martyrs die by other hands,
    and never ever by their own.
"Holy War" is wrapped in bands
    of contradiction, false in tone.

Real martyrdom excludes the deaths
    of wanton killers on the prowl.
They'd enjoy ten million more breaths
    should they, with faith, throw in the towel!

Epitaph for a Palestinian Child

By Michael R. Burch

I LIVED as best I could, and then I died.
Be careful where you step: the grave is wide.

The View from inside ISIS

By Damian Robin

WOW! The wind is blowin', the rain is rainin'
slant across the windowpane—and in
the yard whole oceans storm across the grass
and make some parts too full of mud to pass.
In hours this windblown slop can dry to land
as course and granular as desert sand.

Indoors, most TV feeds disseminate
the propaganda of "Islamic State";
from a few: the snuff pornography;
from most: the sand-march choreography:

semi-automatic publicity
for heated, arid, threat'ning orat'ry,

With sand-drop backgrounds hiding where they are,
on board their all-terrain-adapted car,
boist'rous men shoot heaven with their guns
with chorus lines where no compassion runs.
(There's sometimes footage of explosion clouds,
but where the shelling's gone is kept in shrouds.)

A black flag flaps its silver Arab script
like spores of mercury thoughtlessly tipped.
And ev'ry person in that warring van
has warped inside his head a poisoned plan
of how he'll gnaw the erring world to change,
accepting fear as nothing new or strange.

But look! In the clear blue sky above, a cloud
as white as emptiness, (or stormed seas ploughed
by vast, smooth boats of floating gold) reveals
the hooves of horses leading chariot wheels
with Buddhas, Angels, Ancient Gods, and Saints
sailing through all negative restraints.

Navigating worlds we've never seen,
their forceful wake makes humans bow and lean.
Blinded men drive down a home-less road,
the combatants lift guns aloft to goad,
they run as sand-flecked breezes catch their drifts
and sand blows back and forth in tidal shifts.

I'm sure the chariot has tagged us all.
As local stormy raindrops slap and fall,
our eyes drenched by our blurred humanity,
we cannot know true judgment but can see,
when human deeds are measured Good and Bad,
it's not a get-out clause to shout, "I'm Mad!"

Lines Composed on Salmon Creek

By Bud "Weasel" Rice

May 25, 2015

A LIGHT rain falls
    upon the Western Hemlocks growing tall.
The alders by the flowing creek
    range towering to small.
The white clouds overhead
    are thick and traveling along.
I think of dad and mom
    who tried to teach me right and wrong.
I turn my eyes from outside
    to the mica counter top;
and to my slender, silver-hued computer;
    my eyes drop.
I turn it on and watch
    the screen light up blue, green and white;
and electronic'lly I'm typing
    sentences—quite bright—
against the backdrop
    of the stories on the Internet.
I click my mouse
    upon the image of a fallen jet.

Yemenis claim they have shot
    down a Saudi F-16,
which had conducted raids
    against al-Dailami airbase.
They shot it from the sky
    as fighting rages on the ground.
The Houthi rebels celebrated
    th' aircraft they had downed.
Today's plane crashed,
    as Saudi warplanes carried out airstrikes;
since March one thousand non-combatants

dead beneath those skies.
This news appears
    as backdrop to events in Syria;
four hundred women
    and their children killed in Palmyra,
which follows execution
    of three hundred soldiers there.
Destructive, vicious IS murderers
    create despair.

I look outside and see
    the grass tops touched with silver dew.
Ground cover all around the house
    is green and white and blue.
Beside the branching maples,
    salmon-berry stickers rise.
The swallows are enacting
    Battle-of-Britain dive-bomb fly-bys.
Alyssum flowerets
    and red geraniums fill up
white oval planters on the railing
    near a coffee cup.
Memorial Day is a day
    of peace, away from work;
but not away from all events
    that round the earth occur.
As Candide noted,
    "we must cultivate our garden," for
to cultivate a happy life
    requires more than war.

Chapter IV

Free China,
Free Falun Gong

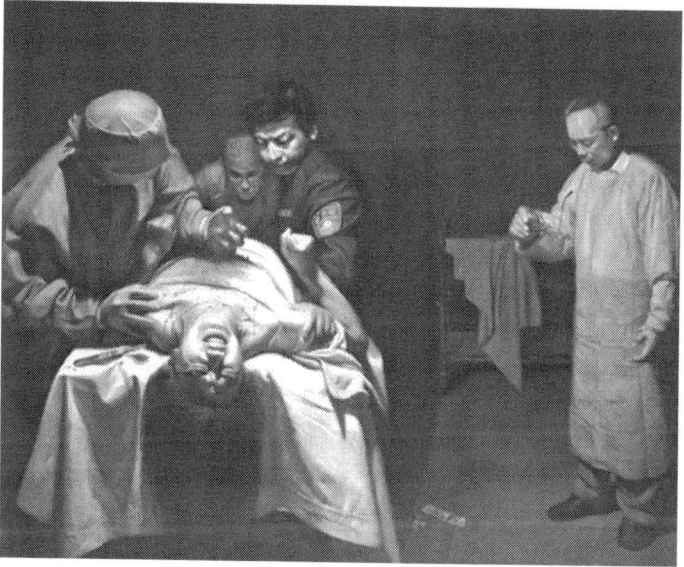

"Organ Crimes," oil painting by Xiqiang Dong. (The killing of Falun Gong practitioners to sell their organs on the international market has been confirmed by the U.S. Congress, Amnesty International, and Freedom House.)

The Red Empire

By Dusty Grein

IN A large East Asian country,
    a police-state occupation
has created cringing terror
    to control the population.
Those who admit Falun Dafa practice,
    face re-education;
without trial they're imprisoned.
    Slavery is the solution
that the Party there has chosen
    as a means of persecution
while inhuman vivisection
    has become an institution.
Now the world we must inspire
to bring down the Red Empire.

Governmental propaganda
    has proclaimed an infiltration;
they have mobilized their forces
    against peaceful meditation,
and the call for full disclosure
    to the people of the nation.
For these crimes there's no admission,
    nor a claim of contribution
in the death of all the victims.
    We must make a resolution
to investigate the reports
    and demand some restitution
for the millions that require
the fall of the Red Empire.

Quieting the citizens
    and stifling their imagination

through both lethal strong-arm tactics,
 and public misinformation.
Tolerance is now illegal,
 when it should be inspiration
for the masses to seek freedom
 and a peaceful revolution.
Basic human rights are missing
 and there is no Constitution,
but to speak these things aloud
 means quick and certain execution;
yet they cannot kill desire
to live without the Red Empire.

Reflections on a Falun Gong Candlelight Vigil

By Shannon Cong / High School Poet

SHALL I compare the CCP
 To a tragic Shakespeare play?
For all the lies of history
 Unfold in China today.

Good and evil set the stage,
 The last and final scene.
But those who 'gainst heaven rage
 Know not of the unseen.

Greater forces are at play,
 Watching this tragedy,
And those who persecute the good
 Will pay eventually.

Black flames of persecution
 That jealousy had fanned

Soon grew and smothered the whole nation,
Thus, Falun Gong was banned.

Those who spoke against the lies
Were killed for their belief.
But who knew mountains would arise
From pebbles of defeat?

Courage is not lack of fear
But how we master it.
For values that they hold dear,
real heroes do not quit.

A single candle burns tonight
A sacred memory.
But soon thousands light up the night
In breathtaking glory.

A flame for every daring voice
That stood against the fiends
A flame to let the world rejoice
When at last this madness ends.

And when the final curtain falls,
The performance is done,
The world will see that after all,
The righteous side has won.

Abuse of Falun Dafa

By Lu "Reed ABCs" Wei

ABUSE of Falun Gong adherents goes on to this day.
The Chinese Communists attempt to make it go away.
They want a permanent solution to their problem, yes,
enforced ideological conversions that repress
and strong coercive measures to outlaw it from the land;
re-education, torture and death too are what is planned.
How many thousands practicing the Dharma Wheel's* spin
of tolerance, compassion, and pure truthfulness have been
exterminated by intolerance and brutal plies?
The Chinese Communists attempt to crush it from their eyes.

**Dharma means "Law" in English and "Fa" in Chinese.
Dharma Wheel literally means "Falun" in Chinese.*

Dharma Wheel

By Sri Wele Cebuda

AROUND the Dharma Wheel spins,
around and round it goes.
It never pauses nor begins,
it simply travels, o!

Though millions fly off from its whirl,
and thousands perish too,
it draws in love from all the World,
the kind, the good and true.

And though some long to stop its turn,
they may as well attempt
to halt the Sun from its great burn
with nothing but contempt.

Tiananmen Square

By Elizabeth Spencer Spragins

A Welsh Clogyrnach

YOUTHFUL zeal fans sparks of unrest
To flames as the jaded protest.
They throng to the square
To challenge the chair
With a stare
To the West.

Unarmed, undeterred, they dare bring
To light fervent hopes for the spring.
The peaceful crusade
Designed to persuade
Draws the blade
Of Beijing.

Red tide swallows the dead and maimed,
Drowns voices, erases those named.
Unmoved by their fate,
Cold eyes of the State
Watch and wait,
Unashamed.

Smoke and Ash

By Katherine Todd

THEY meditated in Tiananmen;
Police "shoot to kill" yet again.
Maybe our world would have regrets
If we pause and follow the cries
Of ongoing pain given rise
By hot irons, lit cigarettes,
To the deplorable torture
Camps by government's order.
We must look, lest we may forget.

The Brave Souls of Autumn

By Rachel Chen / High School Poet

AN AUTUMN breeze blows swiftly through the air,
    And plucks the tree leaves from their humble roots.
Amidst the cold a group stands in the square,
    Its people warmly dressed in hats and boots.

Each face is filled with peace and harmony,
    As soothing music drifts throughout the sky.
Their movements look so tranquil and serene,
    Behind each person faith that cannot die.

Their exercise is suddenly cut short,
    When men in black come storming through the crowd.
They shout with anger, "Orders from the court!"
    The mood is shadowed by a stormy cloud.

These followers of Falun Gong are hurt,
    Though facing persecution, tall they stand.

Throughout their suffering they stay alert,
   They take it all and never raise a hand.

The victims send their thoughts forth righteously,
In hopes that they can all one day be free.

The Bloody Feast

By Pamela Du / High School Poet

Based on the real account of a doctor involved in the Chinese Communist Party's harvesting of organs from innocent living Falun Gong practitioners

IN A bloodstained room on the darkest night,
Four ghastly men enter, draped in white,
Though dripping with sweat their spirits are cold,
Ready to feast with utensils they hold.

They call themselves doctors doing their job,
But really they're thieves, with organs to rob;
The victim is a woman of forty,
Honorable, innocent, and guilt-free.

As the savages tear open her shirt,
A small wooden box falls onto the dirt,
Inside contained a Falun charm and note:
"Mommy, Happy birthday! I love you so!"

Tormented tears swelled in their eyes,
In their wicked hearts, kindness still resides.
Because of their sins, they'll never be free,
Alas, the four men cried out in agony:

"Oh the things we have done to sell our soul,
And invite the devil to take control!"

The Bitter Harvest

By Cheryl Corey

WITH steady hand, he takes a scalpel, cuts
the body open. Liver, spleen, the guts
extracted, packed in ice. The Party man
looks on. There's profit to be made. The plan:
eliminate the Falun Gong and steal
their organs. None will be the wiser. Zeal
of anti-revolutionary thought
destroyed, the statist foe is rendered naught.

A Chinese Man Contemplates Quitting the Communist Party

By Evan Mantyk
After Shakespeare

TO BE a communist party member
    Or not to be, the question looms o'er me:
Is it nobler to accept and suffer
    Its oppression and never be free,
Or t' take a quiet stand and not submit;
    To beat war drums, raise the sharp pen of truth
And sign my good name, declaring "I quit,
    This regime is inhuman and uncouth."

But what do I fear, and what holds me back?
    To lose my job, lose face, or lose my life:
Is all I hold dear what it can attack?
    Is not something in me safe from its knife?

Inside, my spirit cannot be held down;
I sign and wear some invisible crown.

The Organ Harvester

By Reid McGrath

I AM the reaper black and red
   with blood which sticks like chaff to sweat.
I use my scythe on breathing dead.
   It is a scalpel sharp and wet.

I labor in the killing fields.
   I work with deadpanned doctors frank
to see what vivisection yields.
   Our employer: The Organ Bank.

Sometimes I take my mind off it
   and dream of fragrant fields that sway
where a horse whinnies at the bit.
   I am decapitating hay

or mining rubies in the dirt.
   I pluck out hearts and livers live.
It is no use; I cannot skirt
   the bloody Truth—O try! Contrive

some sound excuse for things you do:
   It is a sort of social fête.
Our government I cannot rue.
   I've heard of cannibals who've ate

these very organs. Their dumb slaves
   were sacrificed to fictive gods.
What animals? The vision laves
   my guilt. We're plucking peas from pods.

I help various other folks
   who are not guilty of misdeeds.

The Falun Gong who wear the yokes
  are to these better plants, the weeds!

They should be plucked and shaken, used
  before they march to their demise.
I do not care if they're abused.
  I do not look them in the eyes.

I am the reaper black and red.
  There is no god or souls—I'm told.
There is Social Progress instead.
  One sheep is not worth all the fold.

Toward the Dawn of Truth

By Daniel Magdalen

CONSTELLATIONS beaming kindness,
  Consciences outshining fire,
Shatter the red mists of blindness
  For the lost beneath barbed wire.

Walls shed tears that freeze in stillness…
  Through the haze it's light I'm breathing,
While the vines of hate in shrillness
  Choke the faithless hearts they're wreathing.

Though red acid rain keeps falling,
  To the skyline my thoughts wander—
China's judgment day is calling…
  Truth shall dawn 'midst roaring thunder.

Chapter V

The Preciousness
of Children

"The Wait and The Reward," oil painting by Anna Rose Bain.

Goodbye, Sweet Fetal Child

By Theresa Rodriguez

GOODBYE, sweet fetal child—for you shall die,
　　Because a mother's love is also dead:
The hallowed place of nurture where you lie
　　Shall soon become the ground where blood is shed.
The battle to reject the womanly,
　　Or motherly, for "me, myself and I"
Shall forfeit noble care of progeny
　　(That greater good): hence hearts have gone awry.
The battlefield where "what is hers" to keep
　　Claims hedonistic "choice" its weaponry;
But poison, scalpel, pill or force will reap
　　That fruit, bare yet the casualty.

For those untimely born, it must suffice
That they, not choice, become the sacrifice.

One (1979)

On China's One-Child Policy

By Ron L. Hodges

A POLICY is still in place
　　Which subjugates each woman's womb.
Spin doctors cannot render grace
　　When pregnancy begets a tomb.

Before the mother sees a face,
　　Her green is plucked in fetal bloom.

The thefts till now are hard to trace
   When pregnancy begets a tomb.

Girl babies the males do displace
   Since daughters leave home for their groom;
Thus, men enjoy an honored space
   When pregnancy begets a tomb.

The girls who've died earth can't replace,
   And Truth's cloaked in a red costume.
This program is the world's disgrace
   When pregnancy begets a tomb.

Such evil we need to erase,
   Though shrouded in another room.
We all belong to the same race
   When pregnancy begets a tomb.

The policy goes on apace—
   Its destined death we can't assume—
So battle all must now embrace
   When pregnancy begets a tomb.

Note: Although the Communist regime now has a two-child policy beginning this year, the same inhumane policies of forced abortion and requiring a license to have a child still exist.

Ode on a Children's Cemetery Plot

By Ron L. Hodges

1.

BEHIND the soul-gorged cemetery ground,
  We discovered a plot of yet more dead,
A trim, verdant patch cradled all around
  By a low brick wall, like a toddler's bed.
Sunken in the grassy earth, broken lines,
  Glossy black, marked where all the children slept.
    Tiny toys and small flower bouquets stood
      Among the sunlit stones, saddening shrines
Left by the hollowed hearts that prayed and wept,
  Doubtful life could go on, doubtful it should.

2.

WE STEPPED softly around the little graves,
  Abstractly sharing the parents' sorrows.
I considered how a human behaves
  When tragedy destroys the world he knows—
What happens to a faith in Just power
  When logic fades and chaos seems to reign?
    Each grim gravestone whispered deep words of doubt,
      Yet such uncertainty did not flower
Among these markers of parental pain.
  The monuments' themes were rather devout.

3.

AS I began to read the mournful words
  Etched in stark white upon the sable stone,
Faith and hope seemed the guardian shepherds
  Of their souls: They did not face grief alone.
One young boy, Wyatt, died when he was four,
  Another, Alexa, lived half as long;

Other kids died on the date of their birth.
How were the parents not ripped to their core?
How could they survive? How did they stay strong?
Eyes fixed on Heaven don't plunge through the Earth.

4.

ONE gravestone drew me more than all others.
Like many, it housed an oval image
Of the departed child, but the colors
Were brownish-red, like autumn foliage.
It was an ultrasound of their dead child,
Framed by angels on an ebony face.
This fetal photo shined forth like the moon
At night! Oh, how through shut lids he beguiled
Me with his eyes! What expression of Grace
Could be found in life departed so soon?

5.

WE VIEW random pain as a tragedy,
But chosen pain as a sacred freedom.
This unexplainable loss most moved me
Because, despite what their lives had become,
The seismic collapse of the world they knew,
The parents grasped hope like an ancient jewel,
Not rejecting—but embracing—their God.
The epitaph proved that their faith held true.
"Lord, we give you our Littlest Angel,"
Read the words shining proudly from the sod.

6.

THE feelings hit me like a burst of air
As I imagined myself kneeling here,
Tracing the etchings of a name with care—
My own son's name. How would I persevere?
In a world comprised of mere meat and blood,

I would seek a reunion with the dust.
    But these bedecked stones show that any test
        From a grievous loss to a swollen flood,
Can be passed if we trust the plan is Just;
    Beyond the veil our spirits will find rest.

7.

SO I praise you, child's cemetery plot!
    Though your dark stones stand silent and mournful,
The attuned soul hears words the ears cannot.
    There is a realm of spirit and angel
Beyond the seeming chaos of this life.
    It cradles us with its firm, earthen palm
        Till the time inside these soul sacks is done,
        And we enter Forever, free from strife.
Nursery of the dead, you are a balm
    For my faith, a lasting salve in the sun!

American Monody

By Gregory Palmerino

SECURE the yoke and bind the crown.
Steady the mouth and tongue for sound.
The morning breaks. Our sight is found.
The bell is hung. Let's gather round.

Now strike the lip for their renown.
Each hammer swing is coming round
with darker wind, with darker sound.
The bell is rung. The notes amound.

The body knells. They're going down,
each one a babe into the ground—
each one a babe into the ground.
The bell has rung. Our lives are bound.

If god could hear, his tears would drown
the hell that tolls and hearts that frown.
Instead we hear the dead resound.
Instead we hear the dead resound.

When a Child Dies, the Whole World Cries

By Alan W. Jankowski

TWO young brothers are left at home,
　All by their lonesome selves,
The older one notices a new toy,
　Sitting high up on a shelf.

He climbs up and brings on down,
　What he believes is a toy gun,
He thinks about the games they'll play,
　Boy this sure will be fun.

He aims the "toy" at his little brother,
　And shoots him in the head,
But that gun was not a toy at all,
　And soon the three-year-old is dead.

　　When a child dies,
　　All the stuffed animals cry,
　　Alone on a shelf,
　　They sit by themselves,
　　In a cold lonely room,
　　Like a final tomb.

Johnny's tired of being bullied at school,
　But every dog has its day,
Though all his classmates seem so mean,
　Johnny will make sure they all pay.

The next day at school will be different,
From a knapsack he pulls out a gun,
Suddenly he starts shooting his classmates,
Shoots them in the back as they run.

Soon most of the class has been shot,
And their young bodies are lying there dead,
With one bullet left in the chamber,
Johnny puts the gun to his own head.

When a child dies,
All the angels cry,
The tears flowing down,
On the sad little town,
It's a cold, cold rain,
But it won't numb the pain.

For José this is the biggest day in his life,
It's his gang initiation in the 'hood,
He must seek out a rival gang member,
With a couple of shots he'll be good.

José packs his piece and extra clips,
And his driver takes him to the spot,
He takes aim at his helpless victim,
And another is dead with just one shot.

But that one bullet it ricocheted,
You hear a young mother scream and cry,
As she realizes her young son is hit,
On a cold dark street he is left to die.

When a child dies,
The whole world cries,
All lives matter, big and small,
I ask you people, heed the call,
Please stop the hate, before it's too late,
For the future of us all.

A Child Is Born

By Brian Mc Cabe

TODAY a child is born, into tomorrow's world.
A tiny little mite, around its mother curled;
Is that a smile I see? They tell me it's just wind,
But I look upon your face and I'm the one who grins.

I hope your world is kind, and all your days are glad
For this time is full of woe and many lives are sad;
Let's hope that it improves, in the years which are to come,
And your future is fulfilled in whatever you become.

This world can be unfair, between the rich and poor;
I pray disease and death a distance from your door;
Your fate may be decided by the color of your skin,
But I hope your future rests on what you are within.

Tomorrow is uncertain, in this world in which we live,
But I hope that in your lifetime, you have a gift to give,
The answer to our problems, or a way to carry on
Upon this little earth, third planet from the sun.

A little baby sleeping, as we start a brand new year,
A joyful new born bundle, who as yet knows no fear;
This greeting I address you, whether boy or girl
Take care, for you inherit, our brave Tomorrow's world.

Chapter VI
Love & Other Observations

"Dante and Beatrice" by Henry Holiday (1839–1927)

Valentine

By Michael Curtis

THE name of Spring is ever fresh and fair;
    Her sound is ever gentle, ever true;
The Spring is like the songbird of the air
    Who sweetly choruses the good, the new.

And we, my dear, have often seen the Spring
    Arrive with promise, blossom, fade and go
To who knows where. The bird turns on her wing
    As if to wave to Spring to end the show.

And we have lived to pass another year,
    To watch in course the Spring and sun decline,
Which makes the coming year to me, my dear,
    The more loved, the more precious Valentine.

The snows melt, the flowers open, the songs
Again begin for us a little-long.

To Rest in You

By Michael Curtis

A FAWN is frightened in her bed,
    A sparrow chills in winter's night;
In life we suffer, in life we dread:
    Your love is full, your touch is light,
    We trust in you to do the right.

Each life will turn throughout its course
    From bad to worse, then good again,
Each hopes the good the stronger force:

We each will suffer through the pain
In faith our trust is not in vain.

In all the world of want and need
    I give myself to trust in you;
I cannot know, therefore I plead,
    "Please give me what is best and true"
    I trust, and I shall rest in you.

Valentine

By Reid McGrath

For a girl with rosy cheeks

I DIDN'T know when Valentine's Day was,
and didn't need to. That day came and went
like any other. Now I know it cause
you're perfect, dear; you don't know what you've meant
to me, my life, completely ignorant
to Love which waters a lush Happiness,
as if my rose-like heart were pinched and pent
up in my dry yet sunless parchéd chest.
You have refreshed; you irrigate my heart.
You're water and you're sunshine and you're air
that's unpolluted: cool then warm. You part
the darkness of my isolated lair.
Now fertile is my chest; and a Love grows,
and now you are my Heart; you are my Rose.

The Givers

By Reid McGrath

WE THOUGHT the joy resided in each gift
   received beneath resplendent evergreens
bestrewn with silver tinsel, ornaments
   suspended with gold sequins, angels preened.
Voraciously (while children ached in huts),
   we'd tear the wrapping like greed-blinded squirrels
shucking the shells of indehiscent nuts
   while knowing parents hid us from the world.

We're older now, more generous and glad
   to sit back smiling, watching others lift
a special something we picked out or made,
   slightly embarrassed when we *get* a gift:
knowing already we have more than most.
The true joy is in giving like a host.

Sonnet II

By Justin T. Monelt

THE spark which lights my innermost desire,
   whose flame burns fierce in Spirit and in vein,
your blinding glory makes my heart aspire
   to grasp the highest good one can attain.
Of all the worthy joys that I could gain
   from all the ecstasies of earth's delights,
I'd bask in all the glory of your fame
   before I sink to know those lesser sprites.
And if I'm yet to know those holy heights,
   the strength of which would make my soul a king,

aside your royal passion and your light
    I'd finally come to grasp those greater things.

The world that cannot know of such delight
stands back and trembles lamely at the sight.

The Marriage of Two Souls

By Wilude Scabere

LET me not to the marriage of two souls,
    a man and woman tied eternally,
as time around them rages in its throes,
    do aught but gaze in awe most earnestly
upon their physical commitment; for,
    they've linked themselves together for all time,
and left childhood behind for something more,
    allegiance to the hour, and not the mind.
O, that is harder than most anything
    in life, devotion to a husband or
a wife; because so many things do fling
    impediments 'gainst that embattled door.

All marriage has within its arsenal
are gentleness and love to fight time's squalls.

Ode to a Soldier's Wife

By Dusty Grein

I CAN see your tears are streaming,
    in the lamp light they are gleaming;
How I wish that I were dreaming,
    and that duty hadn't called.
Through the wretched bars we're kissing,
    as the steam train begins hissing
And of all the things worth missing,
    I shall miss you most of all.
Although I am on a mission,
    moonlight on us both will glisten
In the night, just sit and listen—
    love I'll send straight to your hall
    In the night bird's lonely call.

Please have faith and keep on praying,
    in God's grace we'll both be staying.
All the soldiers here are saying
    that the end of war is near.
Though in truth, it would be lying
    if I said I weren't crying,
In my heart, I shall be trying
    not to give in to my fear.
Your sweet smile I'll keep adoring
    in my mind, though it be pouring,
Know my spirit will be soaring
    far above my mortal tears,
    'Til your voice, again I hear.

As I turn, already yearning,
    there's a truth that I am learning—
Loneliness commences burning,
    deep within my broken heart.

Now the captain's voice is urging
　and the engine begins surging.
Frosty air and steam are merging
　as my eyes rapidly dart
Toward the gate, where she is clinging.
　The conductor's bell is ringing.
All the soldiers take up singing,
　as train slowly departs
　While my soul is torn apart.

The Great

By William Ruleman

THE great are often shunned by their own age,
While even the noble dead are sometimes mocked,
And eras are damned when none who sees is shocked
By scads of scorn spat on a sacred page.

Today the sneering cynic's deemed a sage.
The door to love and beauty's never been locked,
Though years have passed when not a soul has knocked
But chose to dwell in a crass comic's foul-smelling cage.

Yet there are those still called to higher things
Than raucous crowds' applause and glib success.
Yes, some know better how to spend their days:

They work to shape a soul that ever sings,
A spirit stirred to soothe, inspire, and bless,
A nature moved to sing and pray and praise.

The Moon

By Michael Harmon

THE moon, a mottled circle cloaked in blue,
As pale and vague as twilight, meant alone
The self I was, the self I barely knew.

For years, before the twilight came in view,
I instigated vain pursuits to own
The moon. A mottled circle cloaked in blue,

I, pale and vague, explored each avenue:
Not one the meaning I had sought, and none
The self. I was the self I barely knew:

Behaving like there never was a clue
Around, pretending I had never known
The moon, a mottled circle. Cloaked in blue,

The moon at twilight hangs in nothing new,
But mottled, pale and vague, cannot condone
The self I was. The self I barely knew

Pursued the unforeseen which only grew
Too late to now with any grace disown
The moon, a mottled circle cloaked in blue:
The self I was, the self I barely knew.

Xerxes

By A.R. Harmon

MY POWER does lie
In hue of the sky
In the refined folds of God's estate.

My throne I have carved
Of sapphire hard
And I crowned it with God's ark of Jade.

My hosts of legions
Number in millions
Like a cloak o'er the land are they spread.

They march ever on
From old Babylon
Across bridges they built from the dead.

So who are these Greeks!
The fools who dare seek
To turn a God's tower to rubble.

Heaven's against them,
My reign has no end
And my sun rests on wings immortal.

Apes or Angels?

By Ron L. Hodges

HUMANS, some say, aren't much more than an ape—
A reasoning beast, quintessence of dust.
Others believe we're of angelic shape.

Hungry for morsels, we scrabble and scrape,
Leaving the tree to indulge termite lust.
Humans, some say, aren't much more than an ape.

Yet not all dwell in this feral landscape—
Their minds are free to transcend what hearts must.
Others believe we're of angelic shape.

We squat under shadows, covet and rape,
Then flaunt our filth like a Renaissance bust.
Humans, some say, aren't much more than an ape.

Still, there are many whose spirits escape
The region where bodies settle for crust.
Others believe we're of angelic shape.

Though such a question makes all skeptics jape,
How could our good rise from matter unjust?
Humans, some say, aren't much more than an ape;
I must believe we're of angelic shape.

Models for Configuring Friendship

By Lynn Veach Sadler

A KNIGHT for whom the Grail is wholly you;
   the one who greets you sans your power, might;
who never counts the favors that accrue;
   adheres to you whatever is your plight.

An audience for fear, for woe, for laugh;
   an egger on, abettor of your best;
the writer, keeper of your epitaph;
   the one who most appreciates your quest.

Your Pythias, your Jonathan, your shield;
   who fiddles first or second at your call;
returns to you at need though far afield;
   would make you Paul, though likes you well as Saul.

If more than three such traits are met, surpassed,
then toast to friendship not to be outclassed.

Blue and Gold

By Neal Dachstadter

MICHIGAN, Michigan: Kings to go forth,
Kerothen, Kerothen, songs to the North,
Ice scattered pond with a trout flipping high,
Geist of beau monde, with a shout to the sky.

Out from the frozen of winter and wrought,
Stout from the chosen, and rendered and sought,
Fathers and Brethren, the future to wrest,
Michigan, *Kerothen*: route to the West.

---

*Kerothen: Greek for "from the heart" / Geist of beau monde:
German and French for "spirit of good society"*

The Circus

By Enri Vilmos

THE band struck up for the comical clowns!
They all sported wigs, red noses, and frowns
And from painted mouths uttered sad cries.
Then the fools threw water and custard pies
In riotous ribaldry: mad, bad, and bold!
The laughter and fun began to unfold;
The children giggled; a vast sea of smiles,
Lucy, and Hanna, and big brother, Giles.

Up above a man swung from a trapeze,
Elegant motion—a leaf in the breeze!
The crowd was silent: a moment to share

High-flying antics with thrills but beware
Of the danger in the nail-biting show:
A truth the artiste must already know?

The magician with a strange box of tricks:
"Hey Presto!" Rabbits, piglets, doves and chicks.
Then a lady in a gown and silk scarf
"Before your very eyes" is sawn in half!

The horses galloped, the lions roared loud;
The ringmaster stood up, regal and proud;
Acrobats stacked high on top of each other:
A pyramid built in a brave manoeuver!
The madcap army in baggy pajamas
Slipped on the skins of sticky bananas,
But danced so sprightly on coconut shells
In elf-toed shoes to the sound of silver bells!

Night's Nuclear Poetry

By Karen Gersch

SO MANY lasers stroked the night,
the sky simply purred and burst apart.
We held our breaths, but not from fright—
the fireworks had launched their start.

Like mad housewives and activists,
the missiles screamed their courses out.
And yet we were amazed and pleased
when globe-sized dandelions shout
their presence, our attention seized
by the panorama we saw unfold
in flaming fans of red white gold.

The air a continual flash and howl,
luminous arcs of sound and light,

a zillion stars machine-gunned through
and splintering the night.

Night's nuclear poetry—so sadly reminiscent
of war—the glare of summer lightning magnified.
Global terrors may be distant,
the lack of care – undignified.

The sky as palette, canvas & hearth.
What boils over sparks into flight
a measuring of what they're worth –
these engineered chips of lethal light.

May artilleries of illusions held
blast harmless passages aloft.
May people learn to feel compelled
to let their deeds and words fall soft.

If something must explode,
let it be this: not skin and
bones and flesh, but this.

An onslaught of firings that end
without corpses or tears,
only wisps of curled smoke
to mark a falling trail of fears.

Offensive Defense;
or, Watching
a Guy Play Ping-Pong

By Reid McGrath

MOST of his offense is steady defense.
   He spins the ball; he grins; he's lightly taxed.
Methodical, stoic, surreptitious,
   he's out for blood and yet he looks relaxed.
Life is largely a battle of attrition:
   he returns all that his opponent smacks
(with too much fury) in his direction.
   Consistently defending—he attacks
his foe's composure: gets beneath his skin.
   He keeps his form while his foe slopp'ly spikes.
Whoever makes the least mistakes will win.
   His type of play not everybody likes.

He doesn't showboat, serve it super-fast;
his greatest talent is that he can last.

The Minuet Ballad

By U. Carew Delibes

THE rustic minuet's small step
   has since been swept away
by all the modern pop and pep
   and fizzle of the day.

One of the first to introduce
   it into music's lair
was Frenchman Jean Baptiste Lully
   of Louis' court and care.

That king first danced it at one of
    his famous, fancy balls.
Of it he could not get enough
    within his brilliant walls.

He liked its bows, he liked its glide,
    he liked its many steps,
to front, to side, to back, to slide
    in graceful, gentle sweeps.

In suites it took its place between
    the sarabande and gigue,
with countless variations seen
    so it would not fatigue.

So as the 18th century
    proceeded on apace,
though many dances left the scene,
    it found a humble place

within sonatas and,
    in classic music keys
of Haydn's, Mozart's, Schubert's and
    Beethoven's symphonies.

So, though it's rarely danced anon,
    it managed thus to stay
because of who it chanced upon
    as it went on its way.

The Curse Called Gangsterism

By Basil Fillis

GAROTTE or gun, or wicked knife—
    with these the gangsters claim their worth.
They're cursed and blind and deaf, and rife
    carcinogens in the womb of Earth.

They're blind to reason, deaf to pleas
    that ricochet off dormant brains.
The dirge of Life (found on its knees!);
    a dirge with endless sick refrains.

The poor are not exempt with them,
    Life's lowest form of predators.
And in our hearts we all condemn
    these self-deluded creditors.

Lamentable laws do promote
    this rot found in the human race.
Give rights to rapists, who take note,
    and rape again. Spit in your face!

They meet with criminal intent;
    which constitutes "attempted crime."
Since "common purpose" gets consent,
    we know our law's not worth a dime.

Far From Home, First Dream in Months

By Andrew Szilvasy

August 13, 2012

I DREAMT last night of singing with Li Po.
  (Or is he now sleeping, dreaming of me?)
How much we drank… The world all vertigo…
  He brought his ch'in. It was life's apogee.

Yet thinking back, if he dreamt me before
  I went to sleep, what would he think? How strange
The beer, steel stools, Beatles' song, pub décor,
  How far from his wooded Eastern Mountain Range!

On a distant tree, a white-crowned sparrow sings.
  Can you too hear it? Or are you still absent?
It's been too long since your last visiting,
  And my time out West has largely been misspent.

Tonight, you won't see Venus; the moon occludes
—O my love, who can bear such starry interludes?

Chapter VII
Translations

"Alexander Pope," oil painting by Michael Dahl (1659–1743). Pope was a prolific translator, known for his translations of the *Iliad* and the *Odyssey*.

The Giant

By Joseph von Eichendorff (1788–1857)
Translated from German by William Ruleman

A TOWER his domain,
    He crouched, a creature caged.
Insane, the weather vane
    Spun round as storm winds raged.

A small hole let him hear
    Rivers' spray and splash;
Bright birds' cheep and cheer;
    Weapons' clang and clash.

With glee a song implored
    The Lord's eternal will.
A wild mob rushed and roared,
    Then all grew deathly still.

Now various voices stray
    Like turbulent sea winds,
Part, join, a mad melee
    He hardly comprehends.

Still, at every sound,
    He feels with shuddering zest
Life, like a giant, pound
    Its path into his breast.

The Forest Maiden

By Joseph von Eichendorff (1788–1857)
Translated from German by William Ruleman

I'M A glowing fire that blazes
Round the rocks' leaf-fringed expanse;
Sea wind's my love, and he raises
Me to a lusty dance
That changes as it churns.
Rising wildly,
Bending mildly
In slim flames' twists and turns;
Don't come near me: this fire burns!

Where the wild brooks rush and glisten
And the towering palm trees stand,
There the stealthy hunters listen:
Deer roam on every hand.
I'm a deer flying through the debris,
High and low,
Where, in the snow,
The last crest gleams silently:
Follow me not: you'll never catch me!

I'm a little bird in the skies,
Soaring o'er the ocean's blue;
Through the clouds from the cliff there flies
No arrow as high as I do;
And the leas and cliffs today,
The woods' solitude
Of such magnitude—
All have fled in wavelets' spray:
For I, alas, have flown away!

How Long the Night

Anonymous Old English Lyric,
circa early 13th century, translated by Michael R. Burch

IT IS pleasant, indeed, while the summer lasts
with the mild pheasants' song …
but now I feel the northern wind's blast—
its severe weather strong.
Alas! Alas! This night seems so long!
And I, because of my momentous wrong,
now grieve, mourn and fast.

Autumn Day

By Rainer Maria Rilke (1875–1926)
Translated from German by Michael R. Burch

LORD, it is time. Let the immense summer go.
Lay your long shadows over the sundials
and over the meadows, let the free winds blow.
Command the late fruits to fatten and shine;
O, grant them another Mediterranean hour!
Urge them to completion, and with power
convey final sweetness to the heavy wine.
Who has no house now, never will build one.
Who's alone now, shall continue alone;
he'll wake, read, write long letters to friends,
and pace the tree-lined pathways up and down,
restlessly, as autumn leaves drift and descend.

Sonnet 3

By William Shakespeare (1564–1616)
Adapted by Alex McKeown

LOOK in your glass and tell the face beheld
  The time has come, dear face, to make another
The same as you, don't swindle from the world
  Its only end, nor blessings from a mother.

Show me a wench who'd leave her womb unsown
  If you would come to till her field! You love
Yourself and lying in a grave alone
  So much? Are your own ends, alone, enough?

You are your mother's and your mother's glass,
  She sees in you her greener years though gray.
Soon, windows smeared, you too some vibrant grass
  Will seek to brighten up a fading day.

He dies who dies alone without a pair,
He lives through death who dies with living heir.

Sommeil, Paisible Fils de la Nuit Solitaire

By Philippe Desportes (1546–1606)
Adapted by Alex McKeown

SLEEP, O peaceful child of lonesome Night,
Alms Father, nourisher of every beast,
Gracious enchanter fading sins to peace,
And, for those spirits blessed, a welcome sight,

God, giving favor to all, all except me,
Why leave me alone? alone charged with this curse?
Even as humid Night drives her blackening hearse,
Whose horses play in ordinary grace and glee?

Where is thy silence? where is thy rest and calm?
Thy dreamings floating like some heavy clouds,
Washing with waves of forgetfulness our cares?

O brother of death, that I could bring thee harm!
I've been calling thee for help, thou art sleeping sound
As I, alert, burn in thy frozen fears.

The Roman Empire Revisited

After Sonnet XXX in Joachim Du Bellay's (1522–1560)
"The Ruins of Rome"
By Reid McGrath

OUR pioneers had felled the forests, burned
the stumps and worked to plough the land with mules.
In those cleared plots the verdant grass that rules
Arcadia had fructified. In turn
sweet-corn would grow. Rocks transformed into walls.
Within those walls they mowed the grain and hay.
They stored the forage for a winter's day
until sly sparks provoked their barns to burn.
So by gradations grew the Empire
till vicious power brought it to its knees:
drew folks to cities, barns consumed in fire,
rock-walls engrossed by pullulating trees...
    Necessity was less than our desire
    and sunk our cities in the flooding seas.

The Lost Artist

After a Fragment of Michelangelo's (1475–1564)
By Reid McGrath

THE soul assays a million medicines
 to no avail. I'm lost in antique woods.
I fought and fought entanglement; but fins
 of sharks and urban mires have withstood.

I now must live with all of these: My boats
 have flaccid sails. My house hasn't a door.
My mind is like an unhinged monkey's
 who's lost his reason inside a junk drawer.

St. John the Baptist

After William Drummond (1585–1649)
Translated by Reid McGrath into modern English

THE last and greatest herald of heaven's King,
 adorned in savage skins in deserts wild.
Staunchly he'd take on what the woods could bring;
 he found them more harmless than man, and mild.
His grub was locusts (grasshoppers). He'd fling
 dead bark aside while honey-bees were riled.
With sun-burnt body, intense eyes, he'd sing
 the psalms of prophets or madmen exiled.

Then he burst forth! "All you whose hopes rely
on God, with me, amidst these deserts learn
repentance and from viperous errors turn!"
Who listened to his voice, obeyed his cry?
 How many of them, on their way, had went,
 while in the caves, his echoes rung, "Repent!"

VIII. Interview

Withstanding the Ravages of Time: An Interview with William Ruleman

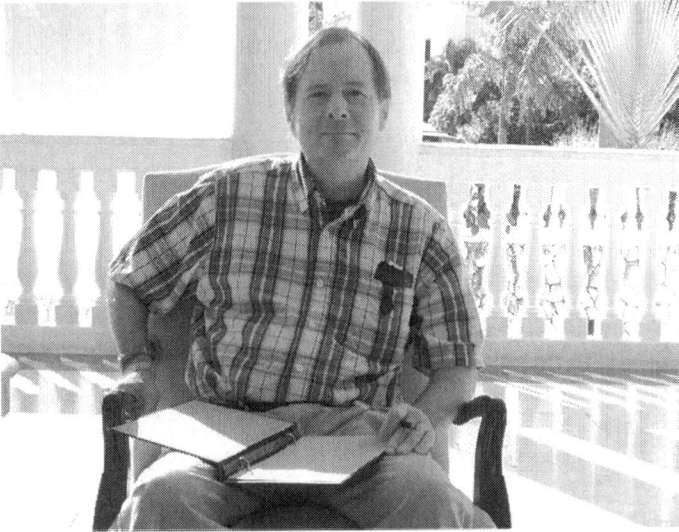

Photo by Elizabeth Sayle Ruleman

By Kristina Pentchoukova

RIGHT from the first email from William Ruleman, I knew that I was interacting with a classicist who upheld traditional English in all manner of communication and behavior. Every email read like a letter. Later, I was honestly surprised by his Southern accent—for some reason, I expected him to have a British accent, so I actually read his emails in a British accent.

I don't normally think about small talk before interviews because it comes naturally, but I started second-guessing myself about whether it would be appropriate to ask him how he was doing, since the British rarely do this, and then I pondered about if it was too cliché to talk about the weather. But again, to my surprise, Mr. Ruleman was the first to ask how I was doing and the first to ask about the weather. Things were off to a good start!

A professor of English at Tennessee Wesleyan College for 22 years, Mr. Ruleman specializes in the poetry of William Butler Yeats. His first two books of poetry were published by Feather Books of Shrewsbury, England, and his translations of Stefan Zweig's (1881–1942) early novellas and stories appeared in 2010 from Ariadne Press.

Question: How long have you been writing poetry?

Answer: Actually, I started late. I didn't really start doing it on a regular basis and in earnest until I was 30. I started out in fiction. I wanted to be a novelist, but when my daughter was born I no longer had the long periods of time for novel writing, and so I turned to poetry and I really enjoyed it. I think it was a wonderful shift for me. Even though I dabble in fiction, I really concentrate on poetry; that's my love. And my love really goes back to early childhood. My mother read me nursery rhymes, and that's where my deep love for poetry began.

I remember writing a poem in ninth grade, and my teacher said, "That's a good poem, you're talented," but I was a boy, a regular boy, and I liked to play sports and I liked to chase after girls, I was in a rock band and so forth, so I didn't pursue it. There were so many distractions. I do remember a poet coming to visit our class when I was in tenth grade. It was the girlfriend of our English teacher, and he asked her at the end of the class, "Does anyone in here look like a poet to you?" and she pointed to me and that seemed to mark me.

Question: What attracts you to the poetry of William Butler Yeats?

Answer: There's just so much rich, deep feeling in his poetry, and there's a great deal of wisdom too. It's wisdom born out of experience and pain and struggle. He talks in one of his later poems about the "foul rag and bone shop of the heart." That is where all of his poetry comes from; it comes from deep pain, it comes from agony, and he takes the unhappy experiences in his life and transforms them into something beautiful. He's just a wonderful poet.

Question: What is the value of rhyme and meter in your poetry?

Answer: They add a music that just sometimes for me is lacking in free verse. They add a richness. They add a depth. They add an extra dimension. So much of free verse is just flat—it just doesn't have music. I did go through a period in which I wrote a lot of free verse. I got to the point where my style was constricting me.

I was very much influenced by W.H. Auden in my early years, and I loved his eloquent style and his wittiness, and he did experiment with a lot of poetic forms, but I think I was too heavily under his influence. And then I got out of writing for a while; and when I went back to writing, my writing was very free, but some of those poems I have not even published yet. Some of them I have gone back to and put them in traditional forms.

There was one I wrote about a great uncle of mine. He used to recite the "Midnight Ride of Paul Revere" when we were children. He wasn't a university professor or anything like that—he owned a hardware store, but he just loved poetry. I wrote an elegy to him, and it was during that free-verse time. I did count it in quatrains, stanzas of four lines, but it was very loose and it was not full rhyme. Over the years I kept working with that until I got into the Tennyson "In Memoriam" stanzas, and it worked, because it was an elegy.

I had to put them into forms that would keep them intact. I want them to last a long time. When I'm just having a conversation with somebody and letting words spill out of my mouth, I'm not expecting those words to last. I'm not expecting them to have resonance or to withstand the ravages of time. There's been so much written that's so silly about traditional poetry being politically conservative; that's a lot of nonsense. There are a lot of people who like traditional poetry who are politically conservative, but it's not a political thing—it's an aesthetic thing. It's also a deeply spiritual thing for me. It's a matter of taste, but it's also a lot deeper than that.

Question: What languages do you translate from?

Answer: I've translated some from Spanish, a little bit from French; I don't get into it that much. I keep peering at it askance and wanting to get deeper into French. German, that's where my concentration is.

Question: What is the value of translating old poetry?

Answer: It's curious how you can read the translations of Homer and they sound more contemporary than reading Chaucer or Shakespeare. It's curious, but it's to resurrect a treasure. The poem is still living, but you want to make it accessible to a contemporary audience and to an English audience.

Spanish is a lot more universal than German, and not as many people know German. There's just a lot in German that people aren't aware of. I just keep finding new poets, and of course the tragic thing is that when people think about Germany they think about Nazism and the Holocaust and all that. But there are hundreds of German poets from before that era, and even during and after that era, totally innocent of all that. And another thing I started noticing when I started reading German Romantics—I got involved with them—is that their tone largely defies what we think about the German character. We think of Germans as being stiff and formal, but there's a lightness and there's a tenderness in so much of the poetry of the German Romantics that's wonderful.

When you translate a poem, you expand the audience for that poem.

Question: How do we make poetry interesting for a young audience?

Answer: I just go into the classroom and I just radiate my love for it, and that's all I can do. I show my love for it when I teach it. Then when I write poetry, it's a bit personal. I don't really think much about an audience. I know there are poets who do, but I write for very personal reasons. I write to speak to those who have come before me and those who coexist alongside of me and those who will come after me.

I don't think of a poem as a riddle, something to be unlocked. There's just so many absurd misconceptions about poetry. I had a friend tell me once, "Well, I know it's not a good poem if I can read it and understand it the first time around." That's just such a sad, distorted view of what makes a good poem. Certainly you do want it to resonate, but you can't predict that. You just have to work with it and make the best living, breathing artifact that you can, and then go on to the next poem.

Chapter IX

SCP Poetry Textbook

A lecture in a knight academy, painted for Rosenborg Castle, in the early 17th century.

Section 1

Basics of Classical Poetry

By Dusty Grein

MOST of us enjoy poetry in one form or another. I am going to lay out the basics of writing classical-style poetry in English, based on standard poetry terms and references. This discussion will focus on classical poetry, that is, rhyming, metered poems.

Please keep in mind that the natural flow of poetic pronunciation and patterns will be influenced by your diction, and sometimes even your accent. This exploration will be done using the diction that comes naturally to me. I am from the Pacific Northwest in the United States, and I speak with no dialect or discernible accent (at least not to me).

Terms

In order to build a poem, and to be able to discuss, explain, and look at samples of poems, we must define some terms. Some of this may sound simplistic, but there are those who struggle with the concepts and I would like to begin with some very rudimentary basics concerning words, sounds, and cadence.

Syllables (Word Building Blocks)

Syllables are single sounds, and the English language comprises words built using these sounds. Some words, "Cone" for example, contain only one syllable (sound burst). Other words, such as "Circle" (CIR-cle), contain two syllables. We have words built from any number of syllables—"Constitutional" has five syllables (CON-sti-TU-tion-al).

Stress (Emphasis)

Syllables are the building blocks of sound that we use to build words, but we don't usually talk in monotone (unless you are attempting to do an impression of a robot). Instead, we vary the pitch, volume, and strength of our pronunciation, or stress, of the syllables in our words.

Sometimes our meaning may be completely different, depending on how we pronounce a single word. For example, if someone says, "How are you *today*?" we can immediately get the sense that something significant happened earlier, probably yesterday. Although more subtle than the use of italics, classical poetry is built using emphasized syllables in patterns that allow the words to flow in noticeable, almost melodic, cadence.

Poetic Feet

This is one of the hardest parts of poetic patterns to grasp, but if you stay with me, and try my tapping methods, you can learn exactly what these words mean, and how we use them to understand and build poems.

Classical poetry in English is usually composed using pairs and trios of stressed and unstressed syllables, in metered rhyming patterns. These syllable pairs and trios are known as poetic feet. Each foot contains a combination of hard (stressed) and soft (unstressed) syllables. In English poetry, there are five basic poetic feet used. Here they are, with their syllable counts and patterns:

iamb—2-syllable foot: A soft syllable, followed by a stressed one, as in the word "adjust" (ah – JUST). Used to create iambic lines.

trochee—2-syllable foot: A hard syllable, followed by a soft one, as in the word "shatter" (SHAT' – ter). Used to create trochaic lines.

spondee—2-syllable foot: Two equally stressed syllables, as in the word "breakdown" (BRAKE – DOWN). Used to create spondaic lines.

dactyl—3-syllable foot: A hard syllable, followed by two soft ones, as in "carefully" (KAYR' – ful – ly). Used to create dactylic lines.

anapest—3-syllable foot: Two softs syllables followed by a hard one, as in "comprehend" (kom – pre – HEND'). Used to create anapestic lines.

There are other patterns of poetic feet, but they are very rarely used in classical English poetry. Here is a complete list of two- and three-syllable feet, with a syllable count and pattern, using "DUM" for the hard syllables, and "dee" for the soft ones. By tapping your finger hard on the "DUM" and soft on the "dee," you will get an idea of the sound stress patterns that can be created.

Syllable Count: Foot Name: Pattern

- 2 syllables: pyrrhus: dee – dee
- 2 syllables: iamb: dee – DUM
- 2 syllables: trochee: DUM – dee
- 2 syllables: spondee: DUM – DUM
- 3 syllables: tribrach: dee – dee – dee
- 3 syllables: dactyl: DUM – dee – dee
- 3 syllables: amphibrach: dee – DUM – dee
- 3 syllables: anapest: dee – dee – DUM
- 3 syllables: bacchius: dee – DUM – DUM
- 3 syllables: antibacchius: DUM – DUM – dee
- 3 syllables: cretic: DUM – dee – DUM
- 3 syllables: molossus: DUM – DUM – DUM

Line Meter

Poetic meter is a count of the number of feet in a line. Most poems are written with between one and eight poetic feet per line. This creates the following poetic metric line types, based on how many feet are in the line:

Number of Feet: Meter Name

- 1 foot: monometer
- 2 feet: dimeter
- 3 feet: trimeter
- 4 feet: tetrameter

5 feet: pentameter
6 feet: hexameter
7 feet: heptameter
8 feet: octameter

Perhaps the most famous type of line is that used by Shakespeare in many of his works, both prosaic and poetic—iambic pentameter—or five pairs of iambs, for a total of about ten syllables.

Often, poets will use a line with a missing first or last syllable for emphasis and strength in their pattern. These lines are referred to as catalectic ("headless").

Rhyme Pattern / Stanzas

The final ingredient in the creation of the classic rhyming poem is the number and pattern of rhyming lines. The final syllable or syllables in the metered lines are set to rhyme with each other in many different patterns, and the number of these lines determines the stanza length.

Stanzas are generally sets of lines that are separated by a blank line. The most common of these are stanzas containing four lines, also known as a quatrain, but there are many varied types of stanzas, from the simple two-line couplet to complex forms like the sonnet or sestina.

Line Length: Stanza Type Name

2 lines: couplet
3 lines: triplet
4 lines: quatrain
5 lines: quintrain, quintet
6 lines: sestet
7 lines: septet
8 lines: octet, octave

In order to show the rhyming pattern in poetic stanzas, I will use the labeling method of describing the rhyming lines using letters so that all lines identified with the same letter rhyme with each other.

Examples

Now that we have a vocabulary, we can examine poetry with a common language. Probably the most common form of poetry, that we learn very young, is the quatrain, in an A B C B pattern. These poems may consist of different meters and feet counts, even having them mixed, as long as the second and fourth lines rhyme:

(a) I loved you before,
(b) I love you still,
(c) I always have and
(b) I always will.

This is a simplistic form of poetry, and it is not truly metered. It is still a valuable form of poetry, and the greeting card industry would be lost without it. For our purposes of exploration, however, we will leave this simplistic approach behind and look at more organized and structured poems. Note that in the following samples, the hard syllables will be bold, italicized, and underlined.

One of the simplest structured poems ever written is a couplet of two rhyming lines titled "Fleas," written in trochaic monometer (a single trochee per line):

Fleas

(a) Adam
(a) had 'em.

Another very popular poem, "A Visit From St. Nick," was written in anapestic tetrameter quatrains (four anapests per line, four lines per stanza) with an A A B B pattern, with the B lines missing the first syllable (catalectic):

(a) 'Twas the night before Christmas and all through the house
(a) Not a creature was stirring, not even a mouse.
(b) The stockings were hung by the chimney with care
(b) In hopes that Saint Nicholas soon would be there.

The last example we'll look at is from Shakespeare's *A Midsummer Night's Dream*. This fantastical play was written in iambic pentameter quatrains (four-line stanzas, with five iambs per line) in A A B B pattern:

(a) And I do love thee: therefore, go with me;
(a) I'll give thee fairies to attend on thee,
(b) And they shall fetch thee jewels from the deep,
(b) And sing while thou on pressed flowers dost sleep;

So now we have a basic grasp on classical poetry terms and forms. In reading the next section, you can examine poems' rhyming patterns and meters, a process known scansion.

Section 2

Ten of the Greatest Poems Ever Written

By Evan Mantyk

IN LEARNING to understand, appreciate, and write poetry, it is paramount to read great poetry. The ten poems selected and presented here represent some of the greatest poems written originally in English and under fifty lines in length. Originally, I compiled these under the title "Ten Best Poems Ever Written" and they appeared in the same order as they appear here, going from least greatest to greatest greatest. Of course, there is ample room to disagree on the order and the selected poems themselves. Nonetheless, what stands is that these ten are definitely among the best left to us by history and have a wealth of poetic genius to share with us.

Educational Approach

These poems provide good, solid education from elementary school to middle school to high school to college. Depending on the level being taught, teachers should prepare to impart level-specific vocabulary, background knowledge, historical information, biographical information, and any literary concepts or devices that they feel are relevant. People studying poetry on their own should prepare to get out a dictionary and dig into history when studying these poems. In any case, it is a good idea to read these poems aloud, read them frequently, and ideally memorize one or more of them.

For all of the poems, there are some basic questions that can be asked of students or of oneself. Analysis I have provided after the poems illuminates the answers to some of these questions, but of course there is much more to also be discovered and savored.

Reading Great Poetry: Questions

1. What **new vocabulary words** did you encounter? What are the definitions? Make sure that they match the context of the poem.

2. What is going on in this poem on the surface? Retell the poem in your own words, line by line.

3. What is the **deeper meaning**, or theme, of this poem?

4. What **literary techniques**—particularly, figurative language (similes, metaphors, personification), rhyme, meter, alliteration, repetition, parallelism, symbolism, and imagery—is the poet using? What effect does the technique you point out have?

5. How does the **historical period** of the poet or biography of the poet increase our understanding of the poem? Or, how does the poem increase our understanding of the historical period or poet's biography?

6. Why is this a **great poem** passed down for centuries?

7. Why is this poem still **relevant today**? Relate it to your own personal experiences or something else outside the poem.

8. What is the **poet's perspective or view**? Do you agree with it? Why or why not?

Activities After Studying Great Poetry

9. Write an introduction to the poem for someone who has never read it before.

10. Memorize one of the poems and dramatically recite it.

The Road Not Taken

By Robert Frost (1874–1963)

TWO roads diverged in a yellow wood,
And sorry I could not travel both
And be one traveler, long I stood
And looked down one as far as I could
To where it bent in the undergrowth;

Then took the other, as just as fair,
And having perhaps the better claim,
Because it was grassy and wanted wear;
Though as for that the passing there
Had worn them really about the same,

And both that morning equally lay
In leaves no step had trodden black.
Oh, I kept the first for another day!
Yet knowing how way leads on to way,
I doubted if I should ever come back.

I shall be telling this with a sigh
Somewhere ages and ages hence:
Two roads diverged in a wood, and I—
I took the one less traveled by,
And that has made all the difference.

Analysis of the Poem

This poem deals with that big, noble question, "How to make a difference in the world?" On first reading, it tells us that the choice one makes really does matter, ending: "I took the one less traveled by, / And that has made all the difference."

A closer reading reveals that the lonely choice that was made earlier by our traveling narrator maybe wasn't all that significant since both roads were pretty much the same anyway ("Had worn them really about the same"), and it is only in the remembering and retelling that it made a difference. We are left to ponder if the narrator had instead traveled down "The Road Not Taken," might it have also made a difference as well.

In a sense, "The Road Not Taken" tears apart the traditional view of individualism, which hinges on the importance of choice, as in the case of democracy in general (choosing a candidate), as well as various constitutional freedoms: choice of religion, choice of words (freedom of speech), choice of group (freedom of assembly), and choice of source of information (freedom of press). For example, we might imagine a young man choosing between being a carpenter or a banker later seeing great significance in his choice to be a banker, but in fact there was not much in his original decision at all other than a passing fancy. In this, we see the universality of human beings: the roads leading to carpenter and banker being basically the same, and the carpenter and banker at the end of them— seeming like individuals who made significant choices—really being just part of the collective of the human race.

Then is this poem not about the question "How to make a difference in the world?" after all? No. It is still about this question. The ending is the clearest and most striking part. If nothing else, readers are left with the impression that our narrator, who commands beautiful verse, profound imagery, and time itself ("ages and ages hence") puts value on striving to make a difference. The striving is reconstituted and complicated here in reflection, but our hero wants to make a difference and so should we. That is why this is a great poem, from a basic or close-reading perspective.

Robert Frost was a New England poet of the late Romantic and Modern periods. He spent his young adult years straddling both farming and teaching in rural New England. When he relocated his family to England to pursue poetry there, his career took off. They returned to New England after three years because of the outbreak of World War I, and he served in many eminent academic positions in the ensuing years.

See page 42 of this journal for a teacher's experience teaching this poem.

The New Colossus

By Emma Lazarus (1849–1887)

NOT like the brazen giant of Greek fame,
With conquering limbs astride from land to land;
Here at our sea-washed, sunset gates shall stand
A mighty woman with a torch, whose flame
Is the imprisoned lightning, and her name
Mother of Exiles. From her beacon-hand
Glows world-wide welcome; her mild eyes command
The air-bridged harbor that twin cities frame.
"Keep, ancient lands, your storied pomp!" cries she
With silent lips. "Give me your tired, your poor,
Your huddled masses yearning to breathe free,
The wretched refuse of your teeming shore.
Send these, the homeless, tempest-tossed to me,
I lift my lamp beside the golden door!"

Analysis of the Poem

Inscribed on the Statue of Liberty in New York harbor, this sonnet may have the greatest placement of any English poem. It also has one of the greatest placements in history. Lazarus compares the Statue of Liberty to the Colossus of Rhodes, one of the Seven Wonders of the Ancient World. Like the Statue of Liberty, the Colossus of Rhodes was an enormous godlike statue positioned in a harbor. Although the Colossus of Rhodes no longer stands, it symbolizes the ancient Greek world and the greatness of the ancient Greek and Roman civilizations, which were lost for a thousand years to the West and only fully recovered during the Renaissance. "The New Colossus" succinctly crystallizes the connection between the ancient world and America, a modern nation. It's a connection that can be seen in the White House and other state and judicial buildings across America that architecturally mirror ancient Greek and Roman buildings, and in the American political system that mirrors Athenian Democracy and Roman Republicanism.

In the midst of this vast comparison of the ancient and the American, Lazarus still manages to clearly render America's distinct character. It is the can-do spirit of taking those persecuted and poor from around the world and giving them a new opportunity and hope for the future, what she calls "the golden door." It is a uniquely scrappy and compassionate quality that sets Americans apart from the ancients. The relevance of this poem stretches all the way back to the pilgrims fleeing religious persecution in Europe to the controversies surrounding modern immigrants from Mexico and the Middle East. While circumstances today have changed drastically, there is no denying that this open door was part of what made America great once upon a time. It's the perfect depiction of this quintessential Americanness that makes "The New Colossus" also outstanding.

Emma Lazarus was a New York poet of the Romantic period. Of aristocratic Jewish background, she worked for the defense of Judaism and Jews in Eastern Europe and throughout the world, as well as for the welfare of immigrants in the United States. Her poem "New Colossus" was at first forgotten among many poems written to help raise money for the building of the pedestal of the Statue of Liberty. After Lazarus's death, the poem was found by statue patron Georgina Schuyler, who selected it to be engraved on the statue. Indeed, the poem is a sort of Lazarus itself, Lazarus being a Biblical character raised from the dead.

Ozymandias

By Percy Bysshe Shelley (1792–1822)

I MET a traveler from an antique land
Who said: "Two vast and trunkless legs of stone
Stand in the desert . . . Near them, on the sand,
Half sunk, a shattered visage lies, whose frown,
And wrinkled lip, and sneer of cold command,

Tell that its sculptor well those passions read
Which yet survive, stamped on these lifeless things,
The hand that mocked them, and the heart that fed:
And on the pedestal these words appear:
'My name is Ozymandias, king of kings:
Look on my works, ye Mighty, and despair!'
Nothing beside remains. Round the decay
Of that colossal wreck, boundless and bare
The lone and level sands stretch far away."

Analysis of the Poem

In this winding story within a story within a poem, Shelley paints for us the image of the ruins of a statue of the ancient Egyptian king Ozymandias, who is today commonly known as Ramses II. This king is still regarded as the greatest and most powerful Egyptian pharaoh. Yet, all that's left of the statue are his legs, which tell us it was huge and impressive; the shattered head and snarling face, which tell us how tyrannical he was; and his inscribed quote hailing the magnificent structures that he built and that have been reduced to dust, which tells us they might not have been quite as magnificent as Ozymandias imagined. The image of a dictator-like king whose kingdom is no more creates a palpable irony. But, beyond that there is a perennial lesson about the inescapable and destructive forces of time, history, and nature. Success, fame, power, money, health, and prosperity can only last so long before fading into "lone and level sands."

There are yet more layers of meaning here that elevate this into one of the greatest poems. In terms of lost civilizations that show the ephemeralness of human pursuits, there is no better example than the Egyptians—whom we associate with such dazzling monuments as the Sphinx and the Great Pyramid at Giza (that stands far taller than the Statue of Liberty), yet who completely lost their spectacular language, culture, and civilization. If the forces of time, history, and nature can take down the Egyptian civilization, it begs the question, "Who's next?" Additionally, Ozymandias is believed to have been the villainous pharaoh who enslaved the ancient Hebrews and from whom Moses led the exodus. If all ordinary pursuits, such as power and fame, are but dust, what remains, the poem suggests, are spirituality and morality—embodied by the ancient Hebrew faith. If you don't have those, then in the long run you are a "colossal wreck." Thus, the perfectly composed scene itself, the Egyptian imagery, and the Biblical backstory convey a perennial message that makes this a great poem.

Percy Bysshe Shelley was an English poet of the Romantic period. Coming from an aristocratic background, he is known for his freewheeling idealism. He broke social and political norms of the time, including marrying below his class, remarrying, opposing monarchy, and opposing organized religion. At the age of 30, while living in Italy, he and a friend died when a storm sank their boat.

Ode on a Grecian Urn

By John Keats (1795–1821)

THOU still unravish'd bride of quietness,
 Thou foster-child of silence and slow time,
Sylvan historian, who canst thus express
 A flowery tale more sweetly than our rhyme:
What leaf-fring'd legend haunts about thy shape
 Of deities or mortals, or of both,
  In Tempe or the dales of Arcady?
 What men or gods are these? What maidens loth?
What mad pursuit? What struggle to escape?
  What pipes and timbrels? What wild ecstasy?

Heard melodies are sweet, but those unheard
 Are sweeter; therefore, ye soft pipes, play on;
Not to the sensual ear, but, more endear'd,
 Pipe to the spirit ditties of no tone:
Fair youth, beneath the trees, thou canst not leave

Thy song, nor ever can those trees be bare;
  Bold Lover, never, never canst thou kiss,
  Though winning near the goal yet, do not grieve;
She cannot fade, though thou hast not thy bliss,
  For ever wilt thou love, and she be fair!

Ah, happy, happy boughs! that cannot shed
  Your leaves, nor ever bid the Spring adieu;
And, happy melodist, unwearied,
  For ever piping songs for ever new;
More happy love! more happy, happy love!
  For ever warm and still to be enjoy'd,
    For ever panting, and for ever young;
  All breathing human passion far above,
That leaves a heart high-sorrowful and cloy'd,
    A burning forehead, and a parching tongue.

Who are these coming to the sacrifice?
  To what green altar, O mysterious priest,
Lead'st thou that heifer lowing at the skies,
  And all her silken flanks with garlands drest?
What little town by river or sea shore,
  Or mountain-built with peaceful citadel,
    Is emptied of this folk, this pious morn?
  And, little town, thy streets for evermore
Will silent be; and not a soul to tell
    Why thou art desolate, can e'er return.

O Attic shape! Fair attitude! with brede
  Of marble men and maidens overwrought,
With forest branches and the trodden weed;
  Thou, silent form, dost tease us out of thought
As doth eternity: Cold Pastoral!
  When old age shall this generation waste,
    Thou shalt remain, in midst of other woe
  Than ours, a friend to man, to whom thou say'st,
"Beauty is truth, truth beauty,—that is all
    Ye know on earth, and all ye need to know."

Analysis of the Poem

As if in response to Shelley's "Ozymandias," Keats's "Ode on a Grecian Urn" offers a sort of antidote to the inescapable and destructive force of time. Indeed, "Ode on a Grecian Urn" was published in 1819, just a year or so after "Ozymandias." The antidote is simple: art. The art on the Grecian urn—which is basically a decorative pot from ancient Greece—has survived for thousands of years. While empires rose and fell, the Grecian urn survived. Musicians, trees, lovers, heifers, and priests all continue dying decade after decade and century after century, but their artistic depictions on the Grecian urn live on for what seems eternity.

This realization about the timeless nature of art is not new now, nor was it in the 1800s, but Keats has chosen a perfect example since ancient Greek civilization so famously disappeared into the ages, being subsumed by the Romans, and mostly lost until the Renaissance a thousand years later. Now, the ancient Greeks are all certainly dead (like the king Ozymandias in Shelley's poem), but the Greek art and culture live on—through Renaissance painters, the Olympic Games, endemic Neoclassical architecture, and, of course, the Grecian urn.

Further, what is depicted on the Grecian urn is a variety of life that makes the otherwise cold urn feel alive and vibrant. This aliveness is accentuated by Keats's barrage of questions and blaring exclamations: "More happy love! more happy, happy love!" Art, he seems to suggest, is more alive and real than we might imagine. Indeed, the last two lines can be read as the urn itself talking: "Beauty is truth, truth beauty,—that is all / Ye know on earth, and all ye need to know." In these profound lines, Keats places us within ignorance, suggesting that what we know on earth is limited, but that artistic beauty, which he has now established is alive, is connected with truth. Truth is, in many cases, connected with the divine. Thus, we can escape ignorance, humanness, and certain death and approach another form of life, approach the truth, and approach the divine through the beauty of art. This effectively completes the thought that began in "Ozymandias" and makes this a great poem one notch up from its predecessor.

John Keats is an English poet of the Romantic period. From relatively humble origins as the son of a horse stable owner to a job as an apprentice surgeon, Keats rose to become a poet of moderate significance in his time, but he died at just 26 from tuberculosis. Posthumously, his poetry, known for its imagery and passion, has been greatly celebrated.

The Tiger

By William Blake (1757–1827)

TIGER Tiger, burning bright,
In the forests of the night;
What immortal hand or eye,
Could frame thy fearful symmetry?

In what distant deeps or skies.
Burnt the fire of thine eyes?
On what wings dare he aspire?
What the hand, dare seize the fire?

And what shoulder, and what art,
Could twist the sinews of thy heart?
And when thy heart began to beat,
What dread hand? and what dread feet?

What the hammer? what the chain,
In what furnace was thy brain?
What the anvil? what dread grasp,
Dare its deadly terrors clasp!

When the stars threw down their spears
And water'd heaven with their tears:
Did he smile his work to see?
Did he who made the Lamb make thee?

Tiger Tiger burning bright,
In the forests of the night:
What immortal hand or eye,
Dare frame thy fearful symmetry?

Analysis of the Poem

This poem contemplates a question arising from the idea of creation by an intelligent creator. The question is this: If there is a loving, compassionate God or gods who created human beings and whose great powers exceed the comprehension of human beings, as many major religions hold, then why would such a powerful being allow evil into the world? Evil here is represented by a tiger that might, should you be strolling in the Indian or African wild in the 1700s, have leapt out and killed you. What would have created such a dangerous and evil creature? How could it possibly be the same divine blacksmith who created a cute, harmless, fluffy lamb or who created Jesus, also known as the "Lamb of God" (which the devoutly Christian Blake was probably also referring to here)? To put it another way, why would such a divine blacksmith create beautiful, innocent children and then also allow such children to be slaughtered? The battery of questions brings this mystery to life with lavish intensity.

Does Blake offer an answer to this question of evil from a good God? It would seem not on the surface. But, this wouldn't be a great poem if it were really that open-ended. The answer comes in the way that Blake explains the question. Blake's language peels away the mundane world and offers a look at the super-reality that poets are privy to. We fly about in "forests of the night" through "distant deeps or skies," looking for where the fire in the tiger's eye was taken from by the Creator. This is the reality of expanded time, space, and perception that Blake so clearly elucidates elsewhere with the lines "To see a world in a grain of sand / And a heaven in a wild flower, / Hold infinity in the palm of your hand, / And eternity in an hour" ("Auguries of Innocence"). This indirectly tells us that the reality we ordinarily know and perceive is really insufficient, shallow, and deceptive. Where we perceive the injustice of the wild tiger, something else entirely may be transpiring. What we ordinarily take for truth may really be far from it: a thought that is scary, yet also sublime or beautiful—like the beautiful and fearsome tiger. Thus, this poem is great because it concisely and compellingly presents a question that still plagues humanity today, as well as a key clue to the answer.

William Blake was an English poet of the early Romantic period. He was also a skilled engraver and artist. Although against organized religion, he was passionately Christian and frequently had visions throughout his life. This latter fact, combined with the unconventional and spiritual nature of his poetry and art, led to his often being thought of as a lunatic.

On His Blindness

By John Milton (1608–1674)

WHEN I consider how my light is spent
    Ere half my days in this dark world and wide,
    And that one talent which is death to hide
    Lodg'd with me useless, though my soul more bent
To serve therewith my Maker, and present
    My true account, lest he returning chide,
    "Doth God exact day-labour, light denied?"
    I fondly ask. But Patience, to prevent
That murmur, soon replies: "God doth not need
    Either man's work or his own gifts: who best
    Bear his mild yoke, they serve him best. His state
Is kingly; thousands at his bidding speed
    And post o'er land and ocean without rest:
    They also serve who only stand and wait."

Analysis of the Poem

This poem deals with one's limitations and shortcomings in life. Everyone has them, and Milton's blindness is a perfect example of this. His eyesight gradually worsened, and he became totally blind at the age of 42. This happened after he served in an eminent position under Oliver Cromwell's Puritan government in England. To put it simply, Milton rose to the highest position an English writer might at the time and then sank all the way down to a state of being unable to read or write on his own. How pathetic!

The genius of this poem comes in the way that Milton transcends the misery he feels. First, he frames himself, not as an individual suffering or lonely, but as a failed servant to the Creator: God. While Milton is disabled, God here is enabled through imagery of a king commanding thousands. This celestial monarch, his ministers and troops, and his kingdom itself are invisible to human eyes anyway, so already Milton has subtly undone much of his failing by subverting the necessity for human vision. More straightforwardly, through the voice of Patience, Milton explains that serving the celestial monarch only requires bearing those hardships, which really aren't that bad (he calls them "mild"), that life has burdened you with (like a "yoke" put on an ox). This grand mission from heaven may be as simple as standing and waiting, having patience, and understanding the order of the universe. Thus, this is a great poem because Milton has not only dispelled sadness over a major shortcoming in life but also shown how the shortcoming is itself imbued with an extraordinary and uplifting purpose.

John Milton is an English poet of the late Renaissance period. He is most noted for his epic poem on the fall of Satan and Adam and Eve's ejection from the Garden of Eden, *Paradise Lost,* which he composed after having gone blind. During his time, he was known for his strong Puritan faith, opposition to the Church of England and the Pope, and his support for personal freedoms. After the English Civil War and the ascension of the

Puritan general and parliamentarian Oliver Cromwell over the Commonwealth of England, Milton was given a high position, making him essentially head propagandist.

A Psalm of Life
What the Heart of the Young Man Said to the Psalmist

By Henry Wadsworth Longfellow (1807–1882)

> TELL ME not, in mournful numbers,
>   Life is but an empty dream!
> For the soul is dead that slumbers,
>   And things are not what they seem.
>
> Life is real! Life is earnest!
>   And the grave is not its goal;
> Dust thou art, to dust returnest,
>   Was not spoken of the soul.
>
> Not enjoyment, and not sorrow,
>   Is our destined end or way;
> But to act, that each tomorrow
>   Find us farther than today.
>
> Art is long, and Time is fleeting,
>   And our hearts, though stout and brave,
> Still, like muffled drums, are beating
>   Funeral marches to the grave.
>
> In the world's broad field of battle,
>   In the bivouac of Life,
> Be not like dumb, driven cattle!
>   Be a hero in the strife!
>
> Trust no Future, howe'er pleasant!
>   Let the dead Past bury its dead!

Act,—act in the living Present!
> Heart within, and God o'erhead!

Lives of great men all remind us
> We can make our lives sublime,
And, departing, leave behind us
> Footprints on the sands of time;—

Footprints, that perhaps another,
> Sailing o'er life's solemn main,
A forlorn and shipwrecked brother,
> Seeing, shall take heart again.

Let us, then, be up and doing,
> With a heart for any fate;
Still achieving, still pursuing,
> Learn to labor and to wait.

Analysis of the Poem

In this nine-stanza poem, the first six stanzas are rather vague since each stanza seems to begin a new thought. Instead, the emphasis here is on a feeling rather than a rational train of thought. What feeling? It seems to be a reaction against science, which is focused on calculations ("mournful numbers") and empirical evidence, of which there is none, or very little, to prove the existence of the soul. Longfellow lived when the Industrial Revolution was in high gear and the ideals of science, rationality, and reason flourished. From this perspective, the fact that the first six stanzas do not follow a rational train of thought makes perfect sense.

According to the poem, the force of science seems to restrain one's spirit or soul ("For the soul is dead that slumbers"), leading to inaction and complacency from which we must break free ("Act,—act in the living Present! / Heart within, and God o'erhead!") for lofty purposes such as Art, Heart, and God before time runs out ("Art is long, and Time is fleeting"). The last three stanzas—which, having broken free from science by this point in the poem, read more smoothly—suggest that this acting for lofty purposes can lead to greatness and can help our fellow man.

We might think of the entire poem as a clarion call to do great things, however insignificant they may seem in the present and on the empirically observable surface. That may mean writing a poem and entering it into a poetry contest, when you know the chances of your poem winning are very small; risking your life for something you believe in, when you know it is not popular or it is misunderstood; or volunteering for a cause that, although it may seem hopeless, you feel is truly important. Thus, the greatness of this poem lies in its ability to so clearly prescribe a method for greatness in our modern world.

Henry Wadsworth Longfellow is an American poet of the Romantic period. He served as a professor at Harvard and was an adept linguist, traveling throughout Europe and immersing himself in European culture and poetry, which he emulated in his poetry. Before television, radio, and film, he rose to become not just the leading poet and literary figure of 19th century America, but also an American icon and household name.

Daffodils

By William Wordsworth (1770–1850)

I WANDERED lonely as a cloud
  That floats on high o'er vales and hills,
When all at once I saw a crowd,
  A host, of golden daffodils;
Beside the lake, beneath the trees,
Fluttering and dancing in the breeze.

Continuous as the stars that shine
  And twinkle on the milky way,
They stretched in never-ending line
  Along the margin of a bay:
Ten thousand saw I at a glance,
Tossing their heads in sprightly dance.

The waves beside them danced; but they
   Out-did the sparkling waves in glee:
A poet could not but be gay,
   In such a jocund company:
I gazed—and gazed—but little thought
What wealth the show to me had brought:

For oft, when on my couch I lie
   In vacant or in pensive mood,
They flash upon that inward eye
   Which is the bliss of solitude;
And then my heart with pleasure fills,
And dances with the daffodils.

Analysis of the Poem

Through the narrator's chance encounter with a field of daffodils by the sea, we are presented with the power and beauty of the natural world. It sounds simple enough, but there are several factors that contribute to this poem's greatness.

First, the poem comes at a time when the Western world is industrializing and man feels spiritually lonely in the face of an increasingly godless worldview. This feeling is perfectly harnessed by the depiction of wandering through the wilderness "lonely as a cloud" and by the ending scene of the narrator sadly lying on his couch "in vacant or in pensive mood" and finding happiness in solitude. The daffodils then become more than nature; they become a companion and a source of personal joy.

Second, the very simplicity itself of enjoying nature—flowers, trees, the sea, the sky, the mountains, and so on—is perfectly manifested by the simplicity of the poem: The four stanzas simply begin with daffodils, describe daffodils, compare daffodils to something else, and end on daffodils, respectively. Any common reader can easily get this poem, as easily as her or she might enjoy a walk around a lake.

Third, Wordsworth has subtly put forward more than just an ode to nature here. Every stanza mentions dancing, and the third stanza even calls the daffodils "a show." At this time in England, one might have paid money to see an opera or other performance of high quality. Here, Wordsworth is putting forward the idea that nature can offer similar joys and even give you "wealth" instead of taking it from you, undoing the idea that beauty is attached to earthly money and social status. This, coupled with the language and topic of the poem, which are both relatively accessible to the common man, makes for a great poem that demonstrates the all-encompassing and accessible nature of beauty and its associates: truth and bliss.

William Wordsworth was an English poet who was a seminal figure of the Romantic period. Along with Samuel Taylor Coleridge, Wordsworth published a collection of short poems, titled *Lyrical Ballads,* addressing often common experiences with common language, effectively breaking from the Neoclassical style that dominated at the time. He rose to the post of Poet Laureate of England.

Holy Sonnet 10: Death, Be Not Proud

By John Donne (1572–1631)

DEATH, be not proud, though some have called thee
Mighty and dreadful, for thou art not so;
For those whom thou think'st thou dost overthrow
Die not, poor Death, nor yet canst thou kill me.
From rest and sleep, which but thy pictures be,
Much pleasure; then from thee much more must flow,
And soonest our best men with thee do go,
Rest of their bones, and soul's delivery.
Thou art slave to fate, chance, kings, and desperate men,
And dost with poison, war, and sickness dwell,
And poppy or charms can make us sleep as well

And better than thy stroke; why swell'st thou then?
One short sleep past, we wake eternally
And death shall be no more; Death, thou shalt die.

Analysis of the Poem

Death is a perennial subject of fear and despair. But, this sonnet seems to say that it need not be this way. The highly focused attack on Death's sense of pride uses a grocery list of rhetorical attacks: First, sleep, which is the closest human experience to death, is actually quite nice. Second, all great people die sooner or later, and the process of death could be viewed as joining them. Third, Death is under the command of higher authorities such as fate, which controls accidents, and kings, who wage wars. From this perspective, Death seems no more than a pawn in a larger chess game within the universe. Fourth, Death must associate with some unsavory characters: "poison, wars, and sickness." Yikes! They must make unpleasant coworkers! (You can almost see Donne laughing as he wrote this.) Fifth, "poppy and charms" (drugs) can do the sleep job as well as Death or better.

The sixth, most compelling, and most serious reason is that if one truly believes in a soul then Death is really nothing to worry about. The soul lives eternally and this explains line 4, when Donne says that Death can't kill him. If you recognize the subordinate position of the body in the universe and identify more fully with your soul, then you can't be killed in an ordinary sense.

Further, this poem is so great because of its universal application. Fear of death is so natural an instinct and Death itself so all-encompassing and inescapable for people, that the spirit of this poem and applicability of it extends to almost any fear or weakness of character that one might have.

Confronting, head on, such a fear or weakness, as Donne has done here, allows human beings to transcend their condition and their perception of Death, more fully perhaps than one might through art by itself—as many poets from this top ten list seem to say—since the art may or may not survive, may or may not be any good, but the intrinsic quality of one's soul lives eternally. Thus, Donne leaves a powerful lesson to learn from:

Confront what you fear head on and remember that there is nothing to fear on earth if you believe in a soul.

Donne, John was a major English poet of the late Renaissance period. While serving as secretary for the Duke of Egerton, he married the Duke's niece secretly and, as a consequence, was briefly imprisoned. He was no longer viewed suitable for public service and spent the next period of his life relatively impoverished. During this period, the couple had many children, while Donne produced many literary works for various patrons. Late in his life, he became a devoted cleric in the Church of England.

Sonnet 18

By William Shakespeare (1564–1616)

SHALL I compare thee to a summer's day?
    Thou art more lovely and more temperate:
Rough winds do shake the darling buds of May,
    And summer's lease hath all too short a date:
Sometime too hot the eye of heaven shines,
    And often is his gold complexion dimm'd;
And every fair from fair sometime declines,
    By chance, or nature's changing course, untrimm'd;
But thy eternal summer shall not fade
    Nor lose possession of that fair thou ow'st;
Nor shall Death brag thou wander'st in his shade,
    When in eternal lines to time thou grow'st;
So long as men can breathe or eyes can see,
So long lives this, and this gives life to thee.

Analysis of the Poem

Basically, the narrator tells someone whom he esteems highly that this person is better than a summer's day because a summer's day is often too hot and too windy, and especially because a summer's day doesn't last; it must fade away just as people, plants, and animals die. But, this esteemed person does not lose beauty or fade away like a summer's day because he or she is eternally preserved in the narrator's own poetry. "So long lives this, and this gives life to thee" means "This poetry lives long, and this poetry gives life to you."

From a modern perspective, this poem might come off as pompous (assuming the greatness of one's own poetry), arbitrary (criticizing a summer's day upon what seems a whim), and sycophantic (praising someone without substantial evidence). How then could this possibly be number one? After the bad taste of an old flavor to a modern tongue wears off, we realize that this is the very best of poetry. This is not pompous because Shakespeare actually achieves greatness and creates an eternal poem. It is okay to recognize poetry as great if it is great, and it is okay to recognize an artistic hierarchy. In fact, it is absolutely necessary in educating, guiding, and leading others. The attack on a summer's day is not arbitrary. Woven throughout the language is an implicit connection between human beings, the natural world ("a summer's day"), and heaven (the sun is "the eye of heaven"). The comparison of a human being to a summer's day immediately opens the mind to unconventional possibilities, to spiritual perspectives, to the ethereal realm of poetry and beauty.

The unabashed praise for someone without a hint as to even the gender or accomplishments of the person is not irrational or sycophantic. It is a pure and simple way of approaching our relationships with other people, assuming the best. It is a happier way to live—immediately free from the depression, stress, and cynicism that creeps into our hearts. Thus, this poem is strikingly and refreshingly bold, profound, and uplifting.

William Shakespeare was an English poet and playwright of the Renaissance period. The most significant figure in all of English literature, Shakespeare's history remains relatively obscure, leaving the door open to countless theories. It is generally accepted that he was not of aristocratic background but rose to become a member of Lord Chamberlain's company of players, known as the King's Men; opened his own theater, the Globe;

and ended his life prosperously. In a long list of acclaimed plays, such as *Hamlet, Romeo and Juliet,* and *A Midsummer Night's Dream,* to name only a few, Shakespeare is often cited for his beautiful language (often in verse form) and his ability to stirringly portray the human experience through his multifaceted characters, universal themes, and brilliant storylines.

Section 3

Writing a Sonnet: Easy to Difficult

By Evan Mantyk

AFTER studying basic terminology and concepts and reflecting on some of the greatest English poetry, it is now time to write our own poetry. We start with the sonnet: the jewel in the crown of English poetry. Depending on the poet's skill or education, you can choose a level that is appropriate.

Put simply, a sonnet is a fourteen-line poem. I'll take you through a simple guide that can lead to a basic sonnet in ten minutes at the easy level to one that demonstrates literary mastery at the difficult level.

"Sunrise on the Bay of Fundy" by William Bradford (1823-1892)

Level 1: Easy
A Sonnet in 10 Minutes

Poetry, at its best, is about those great lofty and universal themes like beauty, the meaning of life, and compassion for our fellow human beings. But, it can also be humorous, unimportant, and topical. The genius of poetry is partially in the ability to convey a lot in a few words and make those few words catchy and attractive to your audience. To write a quick sonnet, we need something specific to focus on: a person, a painting, a book, a character, an event, a place, a relationship between two things, and so on. Can't find a topic? Just look for a picture or poster you like. Here is one of my favorite paintings:

Now, whatever your topic is, imagine it is real. You are in front of it or in it. What are you feeling? Use your five senses and a sprinkle of imagination. Compare what you are thinking of to something ("the water was clear like crystal," "the water was crystal," or better yet "the crystalline water"). You can also repeat words and phrases for emphasis ("*What a* beautiful morning … *What a* gorgeous sea …").

Let the writing begin. Try to limit yourself to lines that are not more than thirteen or fourteen words, and try to mostly end your sentences or thoughts where a line ends. It doesn't have to be one line per thought; you could have a thought that is four lines, for example, but try to wrap it up by the end of that line, not in the middle of it. Capitalization of the first letter of each line and standard punctuation are optional.

Here we go:

On William Bradford's
"Sunrise on the Bay of Fundy"

The waves are bumpy and the wind blows hard,
But the sunrise is so beautiful to look at,
I could sit and look at it forever;
I feel like a new day is beginning and everything is going
To be okay, especially because there is
This guy there for me to talk to.

Why do people, like me, like to look at the water so much;
Why not just look at the land all the time?
There is something special about the water.
Maybe it's the clear horizon line, like a desert.
It makes you feel big and opened up to the sky.
Openness makes you feel cleansed,
Pure, like the garbage can's been emptied,
And powerful, like you could go anywhere.

Done! You have written a sonnet in free verse. Check the timer.

Level 2: Medium
Rhyme-y Poetry

Many people will say that poetry isn't poetry if it doesn't rhyme. Traditionally speaking, this is generally true of short poems like sonnets. Sonnet, after all, means "little song" in Italian, and song lyrics, you might have noticed, usually rhyme.

If you aren't naturally good at rhyming, there are plenty of sources for rhyme words at your local library or online. There are entire rhyming dictionaries. If you can't find a rhyme for your word, the tactic is usually to swap your original word with a different one that has the same meaning. For this, I recommend a thesaurus, similarly found at your local library or online. Or, even rewrite the first line and first rhyme entirely in order to achieve the second line and/or rhyme you want. The rhyming poet must be flexible and agile.

Partial rhymes can also work. For example, the notoriously difficult-to-rhyme word "orange" can be half rhymed with forage, storage, grange, strange, angel, and so on. You can also use alliterative rhymes that focus on the beginning of the word. For orange, you might use oratory, orangutan, ordinary, Orion. Here's an orange poem quickly composed for you:

The Orange Poem

I listened to the oratory
On the topic of the color orange;

> At first I thought it ordinary,
> Someone said "red and yellow make orange,"
> But then it got a bit more strange:
> He said, "A one-hundred-color range
> Forms the continuum of orange."

Ready to rhyme? Next step is your rhyme scheme. (This should be review from Section 1.) If you are a beginner, it is easiest to just rhyme the lines as you go. Lines 1 and 2 end with the first rhyming pair (or couplet); lines 3 or 4 form the next rhyming pair and so on. If you continue this way to the end, the rhyme scheme of your sonnet is expressed this way:

aa bb cc dd ee ff gg

To make it more clear. Here is a quickly composed poem with an aabba rhyme scheme:

> I saw a great big dog (a)
> Standing on top of a log (a)
> I ran away (b)
> But then it came my way (b)
> And said, "May I join your jog?" (a)

The rhyme scheme used by William Shakespeare in the early 1600s was a bit more complicated. This is the typical rhyme scheme for a Shakespearean sonnet:

abab cdcd efef gg

Another classic and more difficult form is that used by the Italian poet Petrach in the 1300s:

abbaabba cdcdcd or abbaabba cdecde

Now, let's return to the first two lines of our example poem on William Bradford's painting. These are the first two lines currently:

> The waves are bumpy and the wind blows hard
> But the sunrise is so beautiful to look at

We'll try for the easiest type of rhyming in which each line rhymes with the next one. After a little shifting and head scratching, we get this:

> The waves are bumpy and the hard wind blows
> But the beauty of the sunrise shows

Continue doing this for each line and you have a rhyming sonnet that looks more traditional than a free verse sonnet. The problem with the free verse sonnet is that people may not see any difference between your poem and ordinary writing, or prose. Rhyming solves this problem quite well.

Level 3: Medium-Difficult
Poetry with Rhyme and Structure

If you want to produce a sonnet with greater elegance and discipline that connects with thousands of years of great poets more fully, then you should consider a rhyme scheme that isn't necessarily so simple. You might use a Shakespearean or Petrarchan rhyme scheme, as described above, or some modification thereof.

Additionally, traditional or classical poets usually adhere to more rigid structure than is found in the easy-level free verse poem. In classical Chinese poetry, for example, each line has the same number of characters. In classical French poetry, poets often count the syllables. Classical Greek and English poets depend on the number and placement of stresses. In most classical cultures, these structures create a kind of universal order, so that any missing word or stress upsets the entire order. Additionally, the sonnet itself matches other sonnets—not only the number of lines, but also the inner structure that has been used in sonnets for hundreds of years. Using a classical model leaves a well-structured poem resonating both backward and forward in history in ways that a free verse sonnet cannot. This is magnificent! Yet, also difficult.

For English poetry, the easiest way to provide some clear structure is by counting syllables, creating what is known as syllabic verse. Not sure how many syllables a word has? Use a dictionary to see clearly how many syllables a word has. Often you can also remove syllables, such as change "mirror" to "mirr'r"; or add syllables people don't normally pronounce, like "poém" (pronounced "poh-EM"). It does not have to be perfect; although, it should tend toward perfection. Sonnets usually have about ten syllables per line (with meter, which we'll discuss later, and this is called iambic pentameter).

Here we go. Our original free verse sonnet is revised to include a Shakespearean sonnet rhyme scheme and ten syllables per line. (Capitalization of the first letter of each line and standard punctuation should be included for this level. Indentation is optional.)

On William Bradford's
"Sunrise on the Bay of Fundy"

Steady currents of wind blow my face,
    Steady currents of water rock my feet,
As the sun rises in its brilliant grace,
    The raucous world seems so smooth and so sweet.

Our small vessel has not yet raised its sail,
    My shipmate and I contemplate the day,
And what our minor journey will entail,
    Nothing so important to again say.

And yet the immensity of the dawn,
    Accentuated by vast horizon,
Is like a giant knot that's been undone,
    And releases each trespass and treason.

Larger and better ships may sail around,
Yet the expanse of my heart knows no bound.

Level 4: Difficult
Sonnet in Iambic Pentameter
and Careful Attention to Meaning

More difficult and rewarding than counting syllables is looking at the meter. The meter is the use of stressed and unstressed syllables to create structure. (This should be reviewed from Section 1.) The iamb is the most standard and natural unit in the English language. It consists of an unstressed syllable followed by a stressed syllable. Iambic pentameter is the traditional meter for a sonnet, and is the most common in classical English poetry in general. You can feel the rhythm of a poem more clearly when it's composed with meter rather than with syllable counting. For iambic pentameter, the rhythm should feel something like "dee – DUM, dee – DUM, dee – DUM, dee – DUM, dee – DUM." Here are some examples:

One iamb: I **am**

Four iambs: I **am** a **man** and **noth**ing **more**.

Five iambs (iambic pentameter): I **am** a **man** who **tries** and **noth**ing **more**

For reference, the opposite of an iamb is the trochee, which is a stressed syllable followed by an an unstressed syllable:

One trochee: **Noth**ing

Four trochees: **Noth**ing **good** can **come** from **ly**ing

In truth, English poets, past and present, often don't stick to meter absolutely. There is also the kaleidoscope of nuances in pronunciations between English dialects, from Texas to South Africa to India, and between time periods and generations. Thus, some balance between the syllabic and metered approach to composing your poem is necessary.

Also important is the meaning behind the words. The sonnet is generally broken up into the first eight lines (the octave) and then the following six lines (the sestet), with the turn (or volta)

in between. The octave sets up an idea, establishing it fully, and then something changes or something different happens with that idea in those last six lines. It is a small journey. Particularly if we look at the Shakespearean sonnet, the sestet could be further broken up into four lines (quatrain) and a concluding two lines (couplet). In this pattern, our fourteen-line sonnet has three distinct sections, going from eight lines to four lines to two lines. Each section is divided by a factor of two, and the second and third sections act to continuously distill the poet's idea down to its very essence.

From this perspective, every single word and phrase needs to be carefully thought over and chosen. Here, there can be no filler words or "yeah, I just put that there because it rhymes." Every letter and comma needs to be working toward the idea and painting it with the clearest colors and most accurate perspective and proportion. Here is our highest and final incarnation of our sonnet:

On William Bradford's "Sunrise on the Bay of Fundy"

A steady wind slaps me on my boat and face,
    And rolling waves try to tip my legs and feet,
Yet, the world of light rises up in grace,
    Which makes my roughshod life seem soft and sweet.

Our ship has not yet raised its measly sail,
    My mate and I have much hard work ahead,
And yet, toward heaven's clouds, blows the gale
    That could lift us up t'where the angels tread,

To where our hearts and minds are freed and cleansed,
    Expanded by the wide horizon line,
To where the softest clouds above ascend
    Into a color free from earth's confines,

Beyond the mighty ships that gather round,
Beyond my flesh, which to the sea is bound.

Level 5: So Difficult It's Easy
The Soundless Sonnet

The ancient Greek philosopher Plato explained that all poetry is a deviation from reality. I have written a sonnet about a guy on a boat. The reality is the boat itself, and the poem is an imperfect and pointless attempt to capture reality. Or perhaps, as Plato suggested, the boat itself is also a deviation from the real boat in the heavens. That means the poem is even further from reality: a deviation from a deviation. The poem is from its first attempt a worse failure than simply getting off your butt and going sailing.

Yet, giving up all art forms is not what I think Plato was getting at. He did support works of art that celebrated the gods and great men. The driving force behind a poem should serve a greater purpose beyond ourselves: something great or divine in nature or purpose. It could be as simple as a birthday gift or a note on a yearbook or as lofty as helping humanity. If there is nothing behind the poem other than our own self-absorbed drive to write poetry and become famous, show off, or feel accomplished, then the poem is, at its very best, unwritten. This is the soundless sonnet, both difficult and easy—which I think Plato hoped he saw more of (meaning, he saw less selfish poetry). This level really works in oscillation with Level 4. Ultimately, it means knowing the right time to write, knowing the lofty and meaningful goals of poetry, and knowing when not to write.

The ancient Code of Samurai, or Bushido, offers some insight on this:

> *Now then, when it comes to the study of poetry, in accord with Japanese custom there have been famous generals and valiant knights throughout history who have mastered the art of composing poetry. So even if you are a warrior in minor rank, it is desirable to take an interest in poetry and even be able to compose the occasional verse.*

> *Even so, if you cast everything else aside to concentrate solely on poetry, before you know it your heart and your face soften,*

> *and you get to look like an aristocratic samurai, losing the*
> *manner of a warrior. In particular, if you become too fond*
> *of this modern fashion of haikai, then even in the assemblies*
> *of reserved colleagues you may tend to come forth with puns,*
> *bon mots, and clever lines. It may be amusing at the time, but*
> *it is something to be avoided by someone who is a warrior.*
> *(Translation by Thomas Cleary / Tuttle Publishing, 1999)*

If we accept the metaphor that life is a battle or war, and we are the warriors, then I think the point here is clear. In my understanding, poetry can never be primary, but only secondary, in the grand scheme of life and the universe. We should continue writing poetry with selfless goals, but know that the greatest poetry has no human words at all.

Section 4

The Importance of Rhyme and Meter

THE following poems and essays explore the importance of classical poetry that has rhyming and meter or form. Here are questions to be asked after reading each:

1. Based on the reading, what is the value of classical poetry?

2. Based on the reading, what are the negative consequences of free verse poetry?

3. To what is classical poetry compared? To what is free verse poetry compared? Provide your own comparison for both.

Why Did Lyric Poetry Die

By Robert King

WHY did lyric poetry die?
'Cause caterpillars cannot fly
And no longer morph to butterflies

Pegasus now has lost his wings
To logic, not to lyric, clings
Concerned solely with words' meanings

Can lyric poetry be restored?
Not unless we hear the words
They'll make beauty as they find their form.

Creativity Requires a Cave

By Reid McGrath

IMAGINE Gretzky "trapped" behind the crease;
    or Pelé, deking, swarmed before the net;
Odysseus before he dons the fleece;
    or Jordan, bodied, ere he stops to set...
It's in tight spaces, when one is constrained,
    when one is challenged, tangled, forced to find
a resolution or a route that's aimed
    forward and not down a path that's blind,
that one can get the best out of oneself:
    creating pathways theretofore unknown.
Rhyme and form are good in and of themselves,
    if not for Song, then also as a cone—

some pylon that we dip around, contrive
so that in some End-Zone we might arrive.

Bound Verse

By Alan Nordstrom

I.

WHY did the classic poets all confine
Themselves to rhyme and meter, line by line,
Whereas today the manner's to be free
Of such restraints, now thought absurdity?

What "free-verse" poets do not understand
Is how exigencies one never planned
Provoke spontaneously new lines of thought
Revealing what one didn't know one sought.

Relinquishing the motive of control
Aimed at some set premeditated goal—
But rather open to the vagaries
Of mind, compelled by the exigencies
Of rhyme, one finds an unexpected place
By what, when fortunately blessed, seems grace.

II.

WHY verse should seek its liberty from beat,
　　Those meters we've for centuries enjoyed,
Then long, as well, from rhyming to retreat
　　As if by such sonorities we're cloyed
I cannot comprehend, for what is left
　　Is tuneless and might just as well be prose
When of all rhyme and meter it's bereft,
　　Devices to keep readers from a doze.
You know with formal verse you're in a game
　　Perhaps like tennis with its lines and net
Where masters over centuries won acclaim
　　Impressing minds with verse they'll not forget.

Why not, instead, enjoy the paradox
Of sonic pleasures that bound verse unlocks?

III.

Bound verse, ironically, is quite unbound,
　　For writing it you have nothing to say,
Since sense comes after you have sought a sound
　　As line by line you pace your measured way.

Perhaps a general notion of a theme
　　Sets off your march across the empty page
As your mind slides into a state like dream
　　Or like a spooky spell cast by a mage.

The form itself provokes this impetus,
   While something in your brain seeks cogency
As each line finds its sonic terminus
   Where sound and sense seem destined to agree.

IV.

The paradox is that by being bound
Your verse allows new vistas to be found.
It's paradoxical that verse that's bound
Gives better access to what is profound
   Than unconstructed verse that rambles free
   Yet can't induce enlightening ecstasy.

Poetry Dies: Influential Artistic Method of Illuminating Human Truth Passed Yesterday

By Ron L. Hodges

POETRY, arguably the most powerful form of communication ever devised by mankind, has died. It was thousands of years old.

Poetry died yesterday after a prolonged illness. Trapped in a meaningless, vegetative state for some time, feeding tubes were removed, allowing Poetry to die with dignity.

Aristotle once wrote, "Poetry is finer and more philosophical than history; for poetry expresses the universal, and history only the particular." And from the time of the ancient Greeks through the middle part of the 20th century, Poetry, through the keen words of rich and poor, sinner and theologian, woman and man, old and young, wrestled universal Truth from the chaos of human existence.

However, after the literary theory of Deconstruction came into vogue among elites, and Postmodernism established its reign among academics in general, Poetry gradually fell out of favor among the general population.

As a consequence of this intellectual revolution, Truth was no longer seen as a goal of Poetry because meaning itself became a form of societal oppression. Truth abandoned as an aesthetic destination, writers began to write obscure, stream-of-consciousness works that defied any interpretation and, at best, merely conveyed some sort of feeling, usually confusion (in fact, the more dumbfounded the reader, the better received the poem).

Long gone were the days in which Poetry, as John Keats said, endeavored to "strike the reader as a wording of his own highest thoughts, and appear almost a remembrance." The reader was no longer a consideration.

Literary elites found this change in Poetry to be liberating: Appealing to readers was creatively stifling—a tool of the establishment to institute uniformity. So they began rooting out any Poetry considered "traditional," "classical," or "meaningful."

However, members of the non-PhD and MFA population mostly rejected this development in Poetry. They looked back with nostalgia on such artists as John Donne, William Shakespeare, John Keats, Emily Dickinson, Langston Hughes, and Robert Frost, the ones whom non-experts could comprehend, enjoy, and perhaps learn from, but few new writers attempted such Poetry, and if they did, they would never appear in a prestigious publication.

Thus, the non-academic of average or above-average intelligence (or even the genius, for that matter) stopped pursuing Poetry. Why, many reasoned, devote time on an activity in which no insight could be gained? And Poetry became a recluse of the Ivory Tower.

Poetry, which had once been one of the great societal influences, was only circulated among elites through select journals, mostly those attached to universities because low subscription numbers were not an impediment to publication; and these elites protected their vision of Poetry dogmatically through creative writing programs. For a short time, Poetry did make some headway into the general population through its "slam" or "performance" variation, but this movement was short-lived.

Ultimately, Poetry written to communicate essential ideas of human existence through vibrant, powerful language was—for all time—a relic of the past. Poetry had become a medium for cleverly worded obfuscation and unattached feeling; it would never mean anything again.

So, Poetry's meaningless existence was ended yesterday.

Poetry is survived by Prose, which still often means something; Poetry joins its siblings, Painting and Sculpture, in death. Cremation is planned.

The Poet as Maker

By James Sale

WHEN you are 62 years old, things may begin to be clearer; you begin to realize to the full extent what territory you are in and demarcating; and I now know what for me is important in poetry and has always been important even as I go back and review work I've written some fifty years ago. For that is the case: I have been writing poetry since I was 13 and really have been a poet since that time. It does not bring in money, although winning Second Prize in the recent Society of Classical Poets' competition got me $100! But it's not about money, but about something much more important.

I was in a residential poetry course some years ago; it was really good. We all had to do some exercise and produce some work and this for me produced a surprising result, for the best and profoundest compliments are those that are unsought, unplanned, and spontaneous; they simply emerge from the universe. So we sat round, about a dozen of us, and shared what we had written. After I had read my short poem out, one woman kindly said, but with a note of astonishment in her voice, "But James, that is real poetry," and having said it the others rushed to agree. (The poem, incidentally, was "Could I But," which appeared in my collection, *To Be a Pilgrim*, in 2011).

It was a strange feeling. Weren't we all writing real poetry? What was different about mine? And there, obviously, was the answer: They had responded to the exercise by jotting down their thoughts and feelings, as one might, and so had written what is sometimes called free verse. Of its kind, it was all worthy stuff—worthy, but unmemorable, and also indistinguishable.

My poetry, by way of contrast, and by way of habit of mind, started with form and structure in mind, because the desire for beauty was also in my mind; beauty without which the whole endeavor is vain. Furthermore, beauty can only come from the patterning of language, from the discipline of language, and not from simply having thoughts, feelings, and ideas and noting them down. There is a powerful therapy to be had in writing down thoughts and feelings, which is a vital healing role for poetry (poetry is associated with the god Apollo, who superintended both poetry and healing); but poetry as high art it is not. So, noting down thoughts and feelings, using line truncation as the sole enabler and signifier that this is poetry, is limited at best.

Free verse is possible, but in reality extremely difficult and near impossible to write. At least, to write well, so that it is returned to again and again like a Yeats or Hardy or Frost poem. The most famous free verse poem of the 20th century, "The Waste Land," by T.S. Eliot is, ironically, full of rhymes, iambic pentameter lines, and structured effects which offset the so-called "freedom" of the lines. I say this because I don't wish to be elitist about poetry. It is for everybody; but not everybody can write poetry. Indeed, Lord Chesterfield observed, "I am very sure that any man of common understanding may, by culture, care, attention, and labor, make himself whatever he pleases, except a great poet." There is a vocation in being a poet, and not all are called, or even many. But my point is this: To write poetry without form is like trying to create a table without tools. Imagine having to construct a chair without a vise, saws, planes, rulers, and other instruments that enable you to fashion exactly what you imagined? Without tools or techniques, we would be shaping the wood with our hands and teeth—we might make something!—and that is how most free verse feels and looks.

People—including leading academics and especially left-wing professors of literature—complain that rhyme is facile, and William McGonagall is always trotted out as the perfect example (as if producing an example of someone who can't create a decent table proved that nobody could!); but that's the challenge: to use rhyme and not be facile when using it. That's what it means to be at least a good poet. Stephen Fry in his wonderful book, *The Ode Less Travelled*, makes the point that the ability to be able to write a sonnet used to be considered the very *sine qua non* of being a poet. Just as using the tools of carpentry effectively is what it means to be a good carpenter; so by analogy, as the lady in the course implied, a real poet uses tools of the language and actively explores their possibilities. Given the range of tools, the choices that we have to use and deploy, there is a wonderful and wide field in which we can operate in order to make the ordinary "wood" into something beautiful and useful like a table. To name just a few of these tools, or techniques, we have meter and the deliberate structuring of rhythm first and foremost; we have rhyme, alliteration, assonance and consonance, and all sorts of sound effects; and we have all sorts of other patterning effects, including line length and acrostics, and so on. However, lest this seem too daunting, it needs to be said that the Pareto principle applies in poetry too: 20 percent of the techniques will create 80 percent of the powerful effects, which is why meter and sound (rhyme being the best example of sound in the English language) are so important.

To write, then, poetry with any degree of power, and to create true beauty without which the effort is vain, requires form and discipline. The word "poet" is etymologically derived from the word in Latin for "maker"; the poet makes. We need, therefore, to encourage all makers of poetry, and all those who seek to find the form for their expression, and use the fabulous tools of the English language to produce that beauty without which, as I said before, the effort is vain.

2016 Poetry Competition Winners

First Prize ($500): Ron L. Hodges, Garden Grove, Orange County, California
"One (1979)" "The Last Column" "Apes or Angels?" "Ode on a Children's Cemetery Plot Part 6"

Second Prize: Bruce Dale Wise, Naselle, Pacific County, Washington
"Lines Composed on Salmon Creek, May 25, 2015" "The Marriage of Two Souls" "Abuse of Falun Dafa" "Dharma Wheel (Falun)"

Third Prize: Daniel Magdalen, Bucharest, Romania
"The Stairway" "Toward the Dawn of Truth" "Meditating at Night"

Fourth Prize: Dusty Grein, Newburgh, Oregon
"The Red Empire" "Ode to a Soldier's Wife"

Essay Prize: James Sale, Bournemouth, England
"The Poet as Maker"

Honorable Mentions
Elizabeth Spencer Spragins, North Carolina
"Tiananmen Square" "Sedona"

Basil Fillis, South Africa
"Counterfeit Martyrdom" "The Curse Called Gangsterism"

Ann Keith
"The Inward Light" "Sonnet on Discernment" "Dawn on the Shore"

Hudson Valley Poetry Prize ($100): Reid McGrath, Ulster County, New York
"The Organ Harvester" "Creativity Requires a Cave"
"Offensive Defense; or, Watching a Guy Play Ping-Pong"

Hudson Valley Poetry Prize Honorable Mentions
Karen Gersch, Orange County, New York
"Night's Nuclear Poetry"

E.P. Fisher, Sullivan County, New York
"Hints from the Moon (Monday)" "Touching Bottom"

High School Prize: Matthew Walton, 10th grade, Shoreline, Washington
"Freedom of Winter Hills" "Laments of the Oppressed"

High School Prize Honorable Mentions
Jarrett Mohn, 11th grade, Kutztown Area High School in Kutztown, PA
"Riverside" "Persecution of the Wiser"

Antoinette Foliart, 11th grade, West Geauga High School in Chesterland, OH
"Squinters" "Buddhist Yoga"

Poets

Agnos, Peter is a poet living in Manhattan in the West 90s with a view of the Hudson River.

Blum, Rick has been writing humorous essays and poetry for more than twenty-five years during stints as a nightclub owner, high-tech manager, market research mogul, and, most recently, "alter kaker." He received first place in the 2014 Carlisle Poetry contest, and honorable mention in the 2015 *Boston Globe Magazine* Deflategate poetry challenge.

Burch, Michael R. edits and publishes *The HyperTexts* at www.thehypertexts.com. His work has been translated into Arabic, Czech, Farsi, Gjuha Shqipe, Italian, Macedonian, Russian, Turkish, and Vietnamese. His poems, essays, articles and letters have appeared more than 1,700 times in publications around the globe.

Canerdy, Janice is a retired high-school English teacher living in Potts Camp, Mississippi.

Chen, Rachel is a high school student at Fei Tian Academy of the Arts in upstate New York.

Cong, Shannon is a high school student at Fei Tian Academy of the Arts in upstate New York.

Corbett, Pamela is a poet living in Bedford Hills, New York. She can be contacted at pamelaacorbett@gmail.com.

Corey, Cheryl placed first in the Dylan Thomas Award category and received honorable mention for the June Kraeft Memorial Award in the 2007 World Order of Narrative and Formalist Poets Contest. Her short story, "The Briar Rose," was selected for *Tall Tales & Short Stories*, an anthology published in 2014.

Curtis, Michael has forty years of experience in architecture, sculpture, and painting. He has taught and lectured at universities, colleges, and museums including The Institute of Classical Architecture, The National Gallery of Art, et cetera. His pictures and statues are housed in over four hundred private and public collections including The Library of Congress, The Supreme Court, et alibi; his verse has been published in over twenty journals. Mr. Curtis consults on scholarly, cultural, and artistic projects, currently: Curator, Plinth & Portal; Co-Director, The Anacostia Project; Vice-President, Liberty Fund, D.C.; Lead Designer on the 58-square-mile city of AEGEA.

Dachstadter, Neal is a poet living in Tennessee. A member of the Demosthenian Literary Society at the University of Georgia, he deployed to Hawija, Iraq, then wrote on Lookout Mountain, continuing with Delta Kappa Epsilon International. Berkeley, Ann Arbor, and Athens encouraged him as a writer. In 2015, he wrote in Arizona at Organ Pipe Cactus National Monument five miles north of Mexico.

Davis, Lorna is a poet who is happily retired and living in California. She can be reached at lornadavispoetry@yahoo.com.

Du, Pamela is a high school student at Fei Tian Academy of the Arts in upstate New York.

Elster, Martin is a composer and serves as percussionist with the Hartford Symphony Orchestra. His poem "Walking With the Birds and the Bones Through Fairview Cemetery" placed first in the Thomas Gray Anniversary Poetry Competition in 2014, and his poem "The Comet Elm" was awarded third place in the Science Fiction Poetry Association's poetry contest in 2015. Email: drumcanine@aol.com

Figueroa, Kathy is a writer and poet living in Ontario, Canada. *Paudash Poems, The Cathedral of the Eternal Blue Sky, Flowertopia,* and *The Ballad of the PoeTrain Poeteer: Winnipeg to*

Edmonton are the titles of her published books, to date, and she's currently adding the final touches to the manuscript for her fifth collection. Kathy can be contacted via email at flowertopia.studio@gmail.com.

Fillis, Basil won first prize in a Poetry Institute of Africa competition in 2000 and third prize the following year. In 2008, the itch to write became unbearable and he ultimately won a third prize at PIA. He is 67 years young and retired. He was born and bred South African.

Fisher, E.P. has published three books, including *Conversation with a Skeleton* and *Out of the Eggs of Ants*. He taught high school English in Uganda as a Peace Corps volunteer and worked for thirty years as a play therapist and adventure-based counselor with special needs children. He holds a bachelor's degree in Literature and a doctorate in Psychology.

Fredericson, Colin is a writer living in New York.

Gersch, Karen is a fine arts painter and illustrator with a BFA from Pratt Institute. Both in painting and writing, Karen's other career and life passion—the circus—figures greatly. She is a Russian-trained acrobat/juggler and clown who now teaches, choreographs and directs across the country. Her art can be viewed at www.artbykeg.info.

Grein, Dusty is a 52-year-old grandfather who just recently became a professional author. He lives in Newberg, Oregon, where a dog named Naked, and his youngest daughter Jazzmyn keep him busy. His website is dustygrein.wix.com/author.

Grey, John is an Australian poet and U.S. resident.

Harmon, A.R. is a traveling writer. She has worked in various locations in Europe and California, and currently resides in New Orleans.

Harmon, Michael holds a B.A. degree in English Literature from Long Island University and B.S. degree in Computer Information Systems from Arizona State University. He is a retired computer programmer and lives in Scottsdale, Arizona. His email address is mjhzen21@yahoo.com.

Henderson, Tony has worked in the music, television and technology industries for many years and also runs a CEO leadership network. He lives in Hampshire, England and his books include *Flat Squirrel: Funny and Absurd Stories about Life* and *The Leopard in a Pinstripe Suit.*

Hill, Ruth was born and educated in upstate New York, and has traveled North America extensively. She is a Certified Design Engineer, lifelong dedicated tutor, and enjoys the spoken word. Over 250 of her poems have won awards or publication in the United States, Canada, United Kingdom, and Israel. She welcomes email at ruthhill@joiedevivregardens.ca.

Hodges, Ron L. is a longtime English teacher, having taught at Oxford Academy in Cypress, California, for the past ten years. He began writing poetry a few years ago. He lives in Orange County, California, with his wife and two sons.

Hughes, Skip writes poetry, and his poems tend to be humorous or iconoclastic or both. His first book of poetry, titled *Chuckleberry Chutney*, is scheduled for publication in the autumn of 2016 by WordTech Communications LLC. He currently lives in Indiana, and previously resided in ten other states and two foreign countries. He has an unusual academic distinction, having attended graduate school at a major state university, in every state beginning with "O." He can be contacted at diffdrumr@gmail.com.

Jankowski, Alan W. is the award-winning author of well over one hundred short stories, plays, and poems. His stories have been published online and in various journals. He currently resides in New Jersey. His book is *I Often Wonder: A Collection of Poetry and Prose*. He always appreciates feedback of any kind on his work, and can be reached by email at Exakta66@gmail.com.

Keith, Ann is a poet whose poems have appeared in various journals (over ninety) as well as in a number of anthologies.

King, Robert is a retired lawyer and poet living in California. His website is theoryofpoetry.com. He is the editor of a book on poetics, *Poetry is – José Garcia Villa's Philosophy of Poetry*, published in 2015 by Ateneo de Manila University Press, Manila, Philippines.

Kurtz, Craig has vexed aesthetic circles since the 1981 release of *The Philosophic Collage*. He resides at the Twin Oaks Intentional Community, in Louisa, Virginia. His website is survivingthedream.blogspot.com.

Larsen, Jason W. is a lifelong Connecticut resident; a toolmaker and machine-tool technician; and a poet, lyricist, and songwriting hobbyist. He can be contacted at jsen2020@gmail.com.

Magdalen, Daniel is a graduate student in the Faculty of Letters at the University of Bucharest, in Romania.

Mantyk, Evan is an English teacher in upstate New York, where he lives with his wife and two children. He is President of the Society.

Mc Cabe, Brian is a retired civil servant in Ireland, who is now pursuing an interest in creative writing, and has had a number of poems and short stories published in Ireland. He writes for a number of journals on the subjects of history and archaeology, and has recently published *Dear Miss B: A collection of Edwardian postcards*.

McGrath, Reid is a poet living in the Hudson Valley in New York. He won First Prize in the Society's 2015 Poetry Competition.

McKeown, Alex is a poet and translator living in Tasmania, Australia.

Mohn, Jarrett is a junior in high school, living in Kutztown, Pennsylvania.

Monelt, Justin T. is a 22-year-old poet living in New York.

Munsell, Mike writes riddles for Riddle Earth, a website he co-founded. His day job is with Greentech Media, where he writes about renewable energy.

Nordstrom, Alan is a Professor of English at Rollins College in Winter Park, Florida. He is the Society's 2012 Poetry Competition First Place Winner. He makes near daily poetry posts of formalist verse on alan-nordstrom.blogspot.com.

Nowicki, Ella is a young poet and aspiring art historian from the Midwest.

Palmerino, Gregory teaches writing at Manchester Community College and writes poetry in Connecticut's Quiet Corner, where he lives with his wife and three children.

Renkoski, Karlee is a student attending the University of Missouri in Columbia, Missouri. Her major is Journalism with an emphasis in Magazine Arts and Culture.

Robbins, Dean is a poet living in Pennsylvania. He can be found on Facebook at *Dean Robbins' Poetry*.

Robin, Damian lives in England. He works as a copy editor and proofreader. He lives with his wife and two of their three adult children. He won Second Place in the Society's 2014 Poetry Competition.

Rose, Hugh is a 22-year-old actor, writer and craftsman. He currently resides in Devon, England, where he helps run programs teaching children the importance of close relationships with each other, themselves and the world around them. He currently takes writing and scripting commissions upon request. He can be reached at hughrose123@gmail.com.

Rodriguez, Theresa is author of *Jesus and Eros: Sonnets, Poems and Songs* and is a classical singer and voice teacher who writes for *Classical Singer Magazine*.

Ruleman, William is Professor of English at Tennessee Wesleyan College. His books include two collections of his own poems (*A Palpable Presence* and *Sacred and Profane Loves*, both from Feather Books), as well as the following volumes of translation: *Poems from Rilke's Neue Gedichte* (WillHall Books, 2003), *Vienna Spring: Early Novellas and Stories* of Stefan Zweig (Ariadne Press, 2010), and, from Cedar Springs Books, *Verse for the Journey: Poems on the Wandering Life* by the German Romantics, *A Girl and the Weather* (poems and prose of Stefan Zweig), and *Selected Poems of Maria Luise Weissmann*.

Sadler, Lynn Veach, is a former college president. She has published five books and seventy-two articles, has edited twenty-two books/proceedings and three national journals, and publishes a newspaper column. Her creative writing includes ten poetry chapbooks and four full-length collections, over one hundred short stories, four novels, a novella, two short story collections, and forty-one plays. She and her husband have voyaged around the world five times, with Lynn writing all the way.

Sale, James FRSA is a leading expert on motivation, and the creator and licensor of Motivational Maps worldwide. James has been writing poetry for over forty years and has seven collections of poems published, including most recently *Inside the Whale*, his metaphor for being in a hospital and surviving cancer, which afflicted him in 2011. He can be found at www. jamessale.co.uk and contacted at james@motivational maps. com. He won Second Prize in the Society's 2015 Competition.

Shook, Don, former president of the Fort Worth Poetry Society and founder of The Actors Company, is a writer, actor, director, and producer. He has performed in theater, film, and television across the country, including opera at Carnegie Hall, New York, and as resident performer at Casa Manana Musicals in Fort Worth and Six Flags Over Texas in Arlington. He is an award-winning author who recently published novels *Bluehole* and *Detour* and four poetry books, and was selected 2009 Senior Poet Laureate of Texas. Don Shook Productions offers shows ranging from murder mysteries to musical reviews: www.shookshows.com

Sokolovski, Maya is a communications specialist based in Toronto, Canada.

Spencer Spragins, Elizabeth is a linguist and editor who taught in the North Carolina Community College System for more than a decade. She can be reached at dragonwithquill@yahoo.com

Szilvasy, Andrew teaches literature outside Boston, and lives in the city with his wife and two cats.

Todd, Katherine is an undergraduate at Kansas State University. She is a double major in English and Secondary Education.

Vilmos, Enri (B.A. Hons) is a poet and musician born in Liverpool, England, who has now settled in the beautiful countryside in the heart of Hungary. As a teacher, he has lectured at schools and colleges in the United Kingdom on 20th century music styles. Meanwhile, he has had two poetry books published, *Uni-Verse* and *Open Wide*.

Wise, Bruce Dale is a poet living in Washington State who often writes under anagrammatic pseudonyms. He won First Prize in the Society's 2014 Competition and is winner of Fourth Prize in the Society's 2015 Competition.

Zwycky, Ben is an English ex-pat now living in the Czech Republic. He has a master's degree in Chemical Engineering and worked a wide variety of jobs before settling down as a freelance proofreader and translator together with his Czech wife, who literally fell into his arms in the year 2000 and with whom he now has five children. He has published two novels, *Nobility Among Us* and *Beyond the Mist*, and one poetry collection, *Selected Verse – Faith and Family*. You can find out more about him and his work at www.benzwycky.com.

Riddle Answers

A South African Riddle by Basil Fillis
Table Mountain

Ten Riddles by Mike Munsell
1. Toilet paper / 2. Paper crane (origami) / 3. Blue /
4. Thumb / 5. Needle / 6. Chalk / 7. Sneeze / 8. Pinky /
9. Skeleton / 10. Chopsticks

Three Riddles by Damian Robin
1. An Argument
2. A Soccer Ball, Basket Ball, Net Ball, Tennis Ball, Table
Tennis Ball, Volley Ball, Hockey Ball, Hockey Puck, etc.
3. A Tunnel, or Entrance to a Subway in the U.S., Metro in
France and Europe, Tube in London, U.K., etc.

Twenty Riddles by Evan Mantyk
I. Canada / II. Armageddon / III. March 31 / IV. Red Sea /
V. Sunday / VI. King David / VII. Purple (or Violet) /
VIII. Orange, Pink, and Green / IX. Pizza / X. River /
XI. Potato Chip / XII. Leaf / XIII. 40 / XIV. 9 Meals /
XV. Duck (or Goose) / XVI. Notebook / XVII. Walmart /
XVIII. Bucket / XIX. Vasco da Gama / XX. Mars

Made in the USA
Charleston, SC
18 April 2016